THE NIGHT CLUB

The Night Club

Herbert George Jenkins

Ahzar Publishing

London
1917

CONTENTS

CHAPTER I FORMING THE NIGHT CLUB 1
CHAPTER II THE COMING OF SALLIE 6
CHAPTER III THE PRIME MINISTER DECIDES TO ADVERTISE .. 19
CHAPTER IV THE BOY 28
CHAPTER V THE BARABBAS CLUB 36
CHAPTER VII FAIL THE NIGHT CLUB 45
CHAPTER VII A SURPRISE BEHIND THE VEIL 51
CHAPTER VIII THE MAKING OF A MAN OF GENIUS 60
CHAPTER IX MRS. BILTOX-JONES'S EXPERIMENT 70
CHAPTER X THE NIGHT CLUB VISITS BINDLE 82
CHAPTER XI THE GENERAL BECOMES A MEMBER 93
CHAPTER XII THE MATER 107
CHAPTER XIII THE ROMANCE OF A HORSEWHIPPING 113
CHAPTER XIV GINGER VISITS THE NIGHT CLUB 123
CHAPTER XV A DRAMATIC ENGAGEMENT 132
CHAPTER XVI THE MOGGRIDGES' ZEPPELIN NIGHT 147
CHAPTER XVII SALLIE AT THE WHEEL 157
DETAILED HISTORICAL CONTEXT 170

CHAPTER I
FORMING THE NIGHT CLUB

The idea originated with Bindle, who is never so happy as when listening to or telling a story. Sooner or later he will so guide conversation as to challenge from someone a reminiscence, or failing that, he will himself assume the burden of responsibility, and tell of how he engineered one of his "little jokes," as he calls them.

"I likes to 'ear 'im tellin' the tale," Bindle remarked one evening, as we sat in Dick Little's flat. Dick had just finished an extravagant and highly-coloured account of an Oxford "rag." "Fancy young gentlemen be'avin' like that," Bindle continued, "instead o' learnin' to be parsons. P'raps that's why they looks such gentle Jims when they gets into a stiff collar," and Bindle buried a wink in his tankard.

A number of us had formed the habit of drifting into Dick Little's flat in Chelsea on Sunday evenings for a smoke, a drink and a yarn. That was in Dick's bachelor days and when he was working night and day at "Tims" (St. Timothy's Hospital). There would be Jocelyn Dare, the writer and inveterate hater of publishers, Jack Carruthers, who tolerated everybody except Mr. Lloyd George, sometimes Tom Little, Dick's brother, and about a dozen others, including a lot of men from "Tims."

One Sunday evening in May, when the air was heavily-scented with blackthorn and laburnum, Bindle and I arrived on Dick Little's doorstep within two seconds of each other.

"Hullo, J.B.," I hailed as he was closing the outer door of the mansions. We always call him "J.B.," following Dick Little's lead.

"Cheerio, sir," he responded, holding the door open for me to pass and, giving vent to an elaborate sigh of relief, added: "I'm glad to get in, that I am. I never feels safe till I gets 'ere. Lord! 'ow them young women do make eyes at me. I s'pose it's the Spring. It ain't safe for me to be out, it ain't really, sir."

We were the first arrivals, and it was during the next ten minutes that Bindle made his proposal.

"Why shouldn't we 'ave a little club, sir, wot does nothink but tell the tale?" he asked.

That was the inception of the whole idea. Dick grasped hold of it eagerly. He is a doctor and doing his best to kill himself with hospital work, and I think he saw in Bindle's suggestion a welcome change after a strenuous week's work. We discussed the matter during the next ten minutes, and, when the other fellows arrived, they were told of the new order of things and, with one voice, acclaimed Bindle a genius. It must be confessed that the men from "Tims" are unrivalled in their capacity for acclamation— they revel in the robustious. It frequently involves Dick Little in difficulties with his neighbours, especially with a choleric old general who lives in the flat beneath.

"I always wanted a night club," explained Bindle when he had disentangled his limbs from the eager hands that had hoisted him shoulder-high. "It 'ud sort o' cheer Mrs. B. up to know that 'er ole man was goin' to 'ell quicker than wot she thought."

After that it was always "The Night Club." We seemed to adopt the name as a matter of course.

We arranged to meet on Sunday evenings at nine o'clock. Each member of the Club was liable to be called upon to tell a story, after being given a reasonable notice.

"Didn't we ought to 'ave rules, sir," enquired Bindle of Dick Little.

"Once you start making rules you are undone," broke in Tom Little, "for you have to frame other rules to modify those already made. At Oxford— — "

"Is it to be a cock and hen club?" interrupted Carruthers.

"A cock an' wot club, sir?" enquired Bindle, pausing in the act of lighting his pipe. "A cock an' wot club?"

"Are ladies to be— — " Carruthers got no further. Bindle deliberately replaced the match in the box, which with his pipe he returned to his jacket pocket. Then with great solemnity and deliberation he rose and walked towards the door.

"Hullo! J.B.," cried Dick Little. "What's up?"

"If you're goin' to 'ave 'ens, sir, this 'ere cock's off, see?"

"Come back, you silly ass," laughed Tom Little.

Bindle paused irresolutely and looked from face to face. "Is it 'ens or no 'ens, sir?" he enquired of Dick Little.

"Why, no hens, of course," shouted Jim Colman, one of Tim's men, giving Bindle a thump between the shoulders that would have made most men wince.

"Right-o, gentlemen; then this 'ere cock withdraws 'is resignation, an' all's serene again," and Bindle returned to his seat and the occupation of kindling his pipe.

Thus it was that women were barred from the Night Club.

The first meeting, however, ended in a fiasco. A fellow named Roger Blint had been called upon to tell a yarn, which proved him to be utterly devoid of narrative skill. It was something about a man who was jilted by a girl and, in consequence, went to the war, returning a few months later with his breast a rainbow of ribbons and his pockets jingling with medals, crosses and stars. We were all much depressed.

After the others had gone Bindle, Dick Little and I conferred together, and it was decided by a majority of two to one that I was first to hear the stories, write them out and read them to the club.

I protested that I was too busy; but Bindle had finally over-ruled my expostulations.

"No, one ain't never too busy to do a little bit more," he said. "I once 'ad a special kind o' performin' fleas, wot was the busiest things I ever seen; yet they wasn't too busy to give me a nip or two now and then. You got to do it, sir," and I felt I had.

We developed into a curiously motley crowd. One night Bindle brought Ginger along, and Ginger had remarked "I don't 'old wiv them sort o' clubs." He refused all other invitations. We had among us a retired policeman, a man who kept a coffee-stall, Angell Herald, the famous publicity agent, the Honourable Anthony Charles Windover (now Lord Windover), and many others. Had we accepted all the nominations, we should have been an uncomfortably mixed crowd. Dick Little was particularly anxious to introduce a "Polish" barber whose name was Schmidt, on the strength of his having exhibited in his shop-window the following notice:—
"I am an alleged Russian subject,"
but we had blackballed the worthy Schmidt.

"Because a cove says a funny thing," remarked Bindle, "doesn't always mean 'e's funny. Sometimes 'e can't 'elp it, poor chap."

As a result of the story about Sallie, Jack Carruthers' sister, she became the only woman ever admitted to the Night Club. There was not a man in the assembly but was desperately in love with her from the moment he heard the tale. Never was a queen more deferred to and fussed over than Sallie. To Bindle she was "the sport of sports." "She ain't always flapping 'er petticoats," he said admiringly. "Yer wouldn't know you 'ad a bit o' skirt 'ere except when yer looks at 'er face."

Bindle was Sallie's cavalier. If the atmosphere seemed to get too thick with smoke, it was he who threw up the window, or propped open the door until it cleared. When Jack Carruthers was not present, it was always Bindle who put Sallie into her taxi; it was an understood thing. One night the Boy, quite unthinkingly, endeavoured to usurp Bindle's prerogative. Bindle had looked him up and down for a moment and remarked cheerily: "All right, 'Mr. 'Indenburg,' you jest wait till I've finished, then I'll come and take you 'ome."

Bindle is a journeyman pantechnicon-man, with an unquenchable thirst for fun. He is small, bald-headed, red-nosed, cheery. To him life is one long-drawn-out joke. He is blessed with a wife and brother-in-law (Alfred Hearty, the Fulham greengrocer), whose godliness is overpowering. Bindle is a cockney by birth and in feeling. He loves mischief for its own sake; but underneath there is always gentleness and consideration for the unfortunate, and a kindly philosophy without which laughter is an insult to life.

Of the other members of The Night Club little need be said. Most of them are doing war-work in some shape or form. Windover is a captain on the Staff, Carruthers is in the R.N.R., Dare is in munitions, his heart "plucked" him for the army, and the rest are doing their bit to the best of their ability. To one and all Sunday is a relaxation from a strenuous week of work, and the presiding spirit of our assemblies is our unanimously-elected chairman, Joseph Bindle.

Although Bindle is a laughing philosopher, he has several streaks of granite in his composition: among them independence. One of the first questions raised was that of drinks. Dick Little, whose generosity is embarrassing, had said that was his affair.

"Very well, sir," was Bindle's comment; "then you breaks up the Night Club."

Enquiry elicited from Bindle the announcement that unless we all paid our share, he "wasn't taking anythink." From that time it became an understood thing that each member became responsible for one evening's refreshments. We had fought Bindle as long as possible, but he was adamant.

It was quite by chance we discovered later that when his turn came to pay, he had worked overtime for a whole week so that Mrs. Bindle should not go short on account of his pleasures.

Bindle had suggested that when the time came a selection of the stories might be printed. It was explained to him that short stories do not sell; the British public does not like, and will not read, them.

Bindle had pondered over this for a while and, finally, had said with decision: "Then we'll make 'em read ours. Me an' Mrs. B. don't neither of us seem to fancy cold mutton, an' when there's a bit over you should jest see wot she can do with it. She can turn it into anythink from stewed rabbit to mince pies." Then turning to me he continued: "You done me proud in that other little 'ymn book o' yours, sir, although 'Earty and Mrs. B. don't seem quite to 'ave recovered from the shock o' bein' famous, and now you can tell all about our Night Club.

"You jest tell about Miss Sallie, sir, ah' Young 'Indenburg, the Cherub (Bindle's name for Angell Herald), an' Mr. Gawd Blast (Jocelyn Dare); why them alone 'ud make any book famous. Then you might add jest a sort of 'int, yer know, sir, that I'd be in it an' then, wot-o!" Bindle did a few fancy steps towards his tankard and took a good pull. "With Miss Sallie, Young 'Indenburg, an' me, sir, you got the real thing."

That settled the matter, and here is the book, short stories disguised as a book of consecutive interest, just as Mrs. Bindle's cold mutton masquerades as "stewed rabbit" or "mince pies." It's a fraud, a palpable fraud, but as Bindle says, we all keep "a-poppin' up like U-boats, that people'll sort o' get fond of us."

Many will say I should have been firmer; but the man who can withstand Bindle when he is set upon having his own way is a being of finer moral fibre than I.

The hour, when it came, for deciding which stories should be included and which omitted, would, I thought, be the last of the Night Club. Nobody agreed upon anything. Sallie refused to allow the story to be told of how she did what the whole power of Germany has failed to do— tricked the British Navy. At the mere suggestion of printing even a covert reference to himself, the Boy became almost hysterical. Angell Herald, on the other hand, felt that all his yarns should go in, and said so, intimating also that he had several others. Furthermore he hinted that he might get us some advertisements to go at the end of the volume, PROVIDED it satisfied him!

Finally it was agreed that Dare and I should decide what stories were to be included, and from our verdict there was to be no appeal. Bindle's last words on the subject were—

"You jest put me an' Miss Sallie on the cover an' you'll see."

CHAPTER II
THE COMING OF SALLIE

When the Night Club was formed it was definitely agreed that it should be for men only, like the best stories and the most delightful women; yet at the third sitting Sallie Carruthers became the one and only woman member. The circumstance was so unexpected that it can be understood only as a result of a thorough description of Sallie, and the difficulty is to know where to begin— the end is always the same, a precipitate falling-in-love with her.

It is all very tedious for Sallie, who does not seem to like being fallen-in-love-with. To use her own expression, "It spoils it." What it is that it spoils she does not seem able to explain, and if pressed she replies despairingly, "Oh! everything."

To a man Sallie is an enigma. She seems desirous of rebuking Nature. She claims from a man comradeship and equality, and he who is not prepared to concede this had better keep out of her way. If some poor wretch, not knowing Sallie's views, happen to be with her in the country and pause to help her over a stile, he never does so more than once. Sallie's eyes will smile her thanks and convey a reproach at the same time. On the other hand, in a drawing-room or at a theatre, Sallie would not be likely to overlook the slightest omission.

There is about her a quality that is as personal as it is irresistible. I have never known her fail to get what she wanted, just as I have never known her to appear to want what she gets. If Sallie asks me to take her up the river on the Sunday I have invited Aunt Jane to lunch, I explain things to Sallie, and there the matter appears to end; yet on that self-same Sunday Sallie and I go up the river, and on the Monday I have a letter from Aunt Jane saying that I am quite right to take every care of an internal chill!

To describe Sallie is impossible. She has very large, expressive, grey eyes, exceedingly long lashes, carmine lips, nondescriptive features, masses of dark brown hair that grows low down upon her forehead, and the quality of attracting the attention of everybody in her vicinity. She dresses well, is the victim of moods, seems to eat nothing, and is as straight as the Boat Race.

With a word or a glance she can annihilate or intoxicate. I call to mind one occasion, when what might have been a delightful dinner was being ruined by a bounder, who monopolised the conversation with pointless stories. Sallie waited her chance.

"I have a grandfather," began the bounder.

"Have you?" enquired Sallie in a tone full of sweetness and meaning.

The man subsided.

One day Sallie rang me up, and by the impatient "There? There?? There??? Oh, bother!" I knew that something important was in the air.

"I am," I replied.

"What?"

"Here, of course," I replied.

"I've got it," said Sallie; "I've got it."

"Heavens!" I responded. "How did you catch it? Hadn't you better go to bed?"

"You're not a bit funny. Aren't you glad I've got it?" she queried.

"Certainly, very glad if you are."

"Jack gave it to me."

"Really? Has he got it too? What is it?"

"A car, of course!"

Now this was characteristic of Sallie. I did not even know that she desired a car; probably her brother Jack, who gives her everything but the good advice she so sadly needs, was as ignorant as I. Most likely he had planned the whole thing as a surprise, just as I once gave Sallie a punt as a "surprise," and learned later that for a month previously she had been taking lessons in punting. But that's just Sallie.

"It's so wonderful," Sallie went on to explain. "It does such funny things. Sometimes it barks like a dog— (I shivered, I knew what that meant for the car)— and sometimes it purrs just like Wivvles." Wivvles is a Persian kitten of no manners and less— — but Wivvles can wait.

At times Sallie is very trying, although unconsciously. She has a habit of taking the first syllable of her friends' surnames and adding a "y." Windover, for instance, becomes "Winny." Poor Graves, who is very fat and moist, she calls "Gravy," and it hurts him just as it hurts dear old Skillington, who is long and learned, to hear himself referred to as "Skilly." It would, however, hurt them both far more if Sallie were allowed to guess their real feelings.

Having to some extent explained Sallie, I must proceed to tell the story that resulted in her becoming a member of the Night Club.

Bindle had arranged that I should tell the first story, and in honour of Jack Carruthers, who is Dick Little's particular pal, and a foundation member of the Club, I decided to tell how Sallie had once personated an admiral's daughter and what came of it.

I

On coming down to breakfast one June morning I found awaiting me a telegram. It was from Jack Carruthers at Sheerness, and read:—

"got hilda here bring malcolm sallie dora for week end cruise meet you sheerness pier four oclock friday jack"

"I'll be damned if I do," I cried aloud.

"I b-b-beg your p-p-pardon, sir?" said Peake, who entered at that moment bearing before him the eternal eggs, bacon and kidneys. Peake is entirely devoid of culinary imagination.

"I remarked, Peake," I replied with great distinctness, "that I'll be damned if I do."

"Yes, sir," he responded, as he placed the dish of reiterations on the table before me; "b-b-b-but you said 'addock on W-w-Wednesdays and F-f-fridays, sir: this is only T-t-tuesday."

"I wasn't referring to fish, Peake," I said severely, "but to Mr. Carruthers and the HILDA. He has invited me to take another cruise with him."

A look of fear came into Peake's eyes. I had recently threatened to take him with me on the next occasion that I sailed with Carruthers. Peake is an excellent servant; but he has three great shortcomings: he has no imagination, stutters like a machine-gun, and is a wretched sailor. For stuttering he has tried every known cure from the Demosthenian pebble to patent medicines, and for sea-sickness he has swallowed the contents of innumerable boxes and bottles. The result is that he stutters as much as ever, and during a Channel crossing is about as useful as a fishing-rod. It has never come to my knowledge that he has sought a cure for his lack of imagination.

"I b-b-beg pardon, sir. I thought you m-m-meant the breakfast. S-s-shall I pack your things, sir?" he questioned, as he stood regarding me wistfully, his hand on the handle of the door.

"What I said, Peake, was that I'll be damned if I do, which does not involve packing. You will not pack my things, and please don't again suggest doing so; it annoys me intensely. That is all."

Peake withdrew with the air of a man who has heard, but does not believe. I was convinced that he was already planning how he should spend his time during my absence. I ate my breakfast in silence, read the shipping casualties to steady my determination to decline Carruthers' invitation, and smoked four cigarettes.

Being unable to get my mind away from the HILDA and her skipper, I determined, therefore, to go out at once and send him a telegram of curt refusal. With my fifth cigarette between my lips I set forth.

The reason for my determination was Dora coupled with Malcolm. Dora bores me, and when Malcolm tries to flirt with her, which he does in a manner that reminds me of a cod making love to a trout, I become demoralised. Dora is Sallie's pal and the wife of some man or other whom I have met and forgotten: no one would think of burdening his mind with anything belonging to Dora that she is not actually wearing at the moment. Dora is extremely modish and regards a husband as she would a last year's frock.

In the Earl's Court Road I encountered Sallie. She was engaged in meditatively prodding with the forefinger of her right hand the lifeless carcass of a chicken. I approached unseen.

"We should reverence the dead, my friend," I remarked gravely. She turned suddenly, with a little cry of pleasure that digested the kidneys and dismissed Malcolm and the HILDA from my overburdened mind.

"Oh, I AM glad to see you," she said, "awfully glad. Can you remember whether a good chicken should be blue or yellow? I know it's ONE of the primary colours, because that's why I remember it?" And she knit her brows as, with a puzzled expression of doubt, she regarded the row of trussed birds upon the poulterer's slab.

"You are confusing the primary colours with the primary pigments. They— — "

"Please try and help me," she pleaded; "I'm so worried. The housekeeper has gone to see a sick relative, and I have to forage for food. It's awful. I hate eating."

Sallie looked so wretched, and her grey eyes so luminous and pathetic, that I took the chickens in hand, purchased two saffron-coloured specimens at a venture, and we proceeded to the fishmonger's.

Sallie's shopping completed, I told her of Jack's wire and my determination.

"Oh! but we MUST go," she said with conviction. "We can't let him down."

I explained that I could not get away.

"I wish I were a man," Sallie sighed mournfully, and gazed down at her very dainty tailor-made skirt, a habit of hers when she wants to engage upon something a woman should not do. Then turning half round and dancing before me backwards, she burst out, "But I should so love it. Do take me, PLEEEEEEEEEASE."

"Sallie," I said, "there's an old lady opposite who is struck speechless by your salvation tactics."

"Oh! bother the old lady," she laughed. "Now we'll go and telegraph."

When I left Sallie, I had telegraphed an acceptance to Jack and wired to Malcolm. Sallie composed telegrams, which must have caused them some surprise on account of their extreme cordiality. We then parted, Sallie to call on Dora, I to telephone to Peake that he might after all pack my bag, although there were three days in which to do it. As a matter of fact I did not feel equal to that I-never-doubted-you'd-go-sir look in his eyes.

II

Victoria Station had been agreed upon as the rendezvous, and there we met. Sallie looked demurely trim and appropriately dressed. Dora seemed to have got confused between a yachting-trip and a garden-party, and had struck an unhappy medium between the two. Dora has what is known to women as "a French figure"; but what to man remains a mystery; she also has fair hair and a something in the eye that makes men look at her with interest and women with disapproval.

Malcolm is all legs and arms and sketch-book. He was quite appropriately dressed in a Norfolk knickerbocker suit, with a straw hat and an umbrella— appropriately dressed, that is, for anything but yachting. Malcolm is a marine-painter, and what he does not know about the sea and boats need not concern either yachtsman or artist. He is tall and thin, with the temper of an angel, the caution of a good sailor and the courage of a lion. He waves his arms about like semaphores, rates woman lower than a barge, and never fails to earn the respect of sailormen.

Malcolm is a man of strange capacities and curious limitations. Anybody will do anything for him, porters carry his luggage with no thought of tips, editors publish his drawings, whether they want to or no, people purchase his pictures without in the least understanding them, and, finally, everybody accepts him without comment, much as they do a Bank Holiday or an eclipse.

Sallie and Dora between them had only a small valise, whereas Malcolm carried a sketch-book and an umbrella. He, as I, was depending upon Carruthers for all save a tooth-brush.

There was the inevitable delay on the line, and we were over an hour late. Sallie was in a fever of excitement lest the HILDA should sail without us. Malcolm, with that supreme lack of tact so characteristic of him, explained what a ticklish business it was getting out of Sheerness Harbour under sail with the wind in its present quarter. He thought that in all probability the auxiliary motor had broken down, and that the HILDA would have to depend upon canvas to get out, in which case she must have sailed half-an-hour before.

When we eventually drew into the station, out of the train, down the platform, through the gates, into the street, sped Malcolm, and we, like "panting time toiled after him in vain." He waved his umbrella to us to hurry, not knowing that Dora has a deplorably short wind. On he tore, and finally disappeared through the pier-gates without, as we afterwards found, paying his toll, a privilege he had generously delegated to us. When we in turn passed through the gates, it was to find Malcolm hysterically waving his umbrella, apparently at the Medway guardship. Suddenly the truth dawned upon us, the HILDA had sailed. Probably Carruthers had not received the telegram.

Arrived at the pierhead we saw the HILDA off the Isle of Grain, two miles distant, slowly slipping out of the Medway against the tide with the aid of her auxiliary motor. The sight was one of the most depressing that I have ever experienced. We looked at each other blankly.

"It's the cup of Tantalus," I murmured, with classical resignation.

"It's that damned auxiliary motor," muttered the practical Malcolm.

"Commong faire?" enquired Dora, who is inclined occasionally to lapse into French on the strength of her figure. "Commong faire?"

"Noo verrong," replied Malcolm in what he conceives to be the Gallic tongue.

I made no remark, but with Sallie stood idly watching a steam-pinnace approaching the pier-head from the Medway guardship that lay moored directly opposite.

"I know!" Sallie suddenly said, and I knew that she really did know. There are moments when I am at a loss to understand why I do not run away with Sallie and marry her in spite of herself, merely as a speculative investment. She is exquisitely ornamental, and her utility equals her æsthetic qualities; more would be impossible.

At Sallie's exclamation Dora and Malcolm drew towards us.

"Tell me the name of an admiral," Sallie cried, her large, grey eyes diverted from epic contemplation of the universe to a lyric mischievousness. "I want an admiral."

"Try a lieutenant to begin with," Malcolm suggested, and was withered.

"An admiral," said Dora. "Nelson; he was an admiral, wasn't— — ?"

"Van Tromp, Blake, Benbow, Villeneuve, Collingwood, St. Vincent, Cochrane— — " glibly responded Malcolm.

As the responses were uttered at the same time, Sallie probably heard little of what was said. Suddenly becoming very calm, she addressed herself to Malcolm.

"I want to know the name of an English admiral of the present day. Are there any?"

"Plenty," responded Malcolm. "Crosstrees (I dare not give the real name), First Sea Lord, May, Meux, Jellicoe, Beresford, Scott, Beatty."

"Is Admiral Crosstrees married?" queried Sallie calmly. "Has he grown-up daughters? Is he old?"

"Any First Sea Lord who has not grown-up daughters has evaded his responsibilities as an officer and a gentleman," I remarked.

Suddenly Sallie took command. Motioning us back, she went to the extreme end of the pier and looked down. A moment later, the white top of a naval cap appeared above the edge, followed by a fair face and five feet six of a sub-lieutenant. Sallie addressed herself to him, and, taking advantage of his obvious confusion, said: "Will you please take us out to that yacht," pointing to the HILDA. "She has gone without us, and— — well, we want to get on board."

When the sub. had recovered from Sallie's smile and her carnation tint, he stammered his regret.

"I'm most awfully sorry; but I'm here to take liberty men aboard. I'm, I'm, afraid I can't, otherwise I would with er— er— er— — "

"What are liberty men?" questioned Sallie, looking at him with grey-eyed gravity.

"Men who have been ashore on leave," was the response.

"Can you signal to that?" asked Sallie with guile, nodding at the guardship.

"I beg pardon," replied the bewildered sub, fast breaking up beneath Sallie's gaze.

"Does the captain know the First Sea Lord, Admiral Crosstrees?"

"I— I don't know," he replied, "I— — "

"I am Miss Crosstrees. Will you please tell me who you are. I should like to know, because you are the first officer I have met who has been discourteous to me. I will not trouble you further," and she moved away like an outraged Mrs. Siddons.

"I— I'm awfully sorry, Miss Crosstrees. I didn't know— — of course— — if you can get down. I will most certainly— — " He collapsed into confused silence.

"You will take us then?" Sallie questioned, approaching two steps nearer to him.

"Certainly: but er— er— can you— er?"

Sallie looked down. A perpendicular iron ladder led down to the pinnace some thirty feet below. It was not pleasant for a woman.

"Will you go down and— and— — " faltered Sallie. He was a nice youth, who understood and disappeared, I after him. Then came Sallie, easily and naturally as if accustomed to such ladders all her life. Dora followed, almost hysterical with fear, and finally came Malcolm, with his umbrella and the valise in one hand and his sketch-book between his teeth. I could see the men were impressed with his performance.

I did not at all like the adventure. It might end very unpleasantly for some of us, and the "some," I knew, would be Malcolm and me. I was by no means reassured when I saw that the sub. was steering the pinnace directly for the guardship. Did he suspect? I racked my brains to try and recollect if the First Sea Lord were married, if he had a family, if— — . It was as if from far away that I heard the sub, hailing the guardship through a megaphone.

"Admiral Crosstrees' daughter wishes to be put aboard that yacht, sir. Am I— — "

"Certainly," came the reply, as the officer of the watch came to the side and saluted. Hands bobbed up from everywhere, and it seemed as if a dead ship had suddenly been galvanised into life. Sallie's bow and smile were much appreciated, every man taking it unto himself. That is Sallie's way. She can slay a regiment or a ship's company with a glance, whilst another woman is exhausting herself in trying to enlist the interest of a stockbroker.

Out we rushed after the HILDA. Sallie, now that she had gained her point, became absorbed in contemplating the Isle of Grain, and watching the white wake of the pinnace. Occasionally a slight, half-sad, half-contemplative smile would flit across her features. She had forgotten everything— yachts, pinnaces, subs, and was just alone with the things that mattered, the sea, the sky, and the green fields.

Dora chatted with the sub., whose eyes repeatedly wandered to where Sallie was standing quite oblivious to his presence. Malcolm was in deep converse with one of the crew, whilst I watched the others, especially Sallie. I find it difficult to keep my eyes off Sallie when she is within their range. She is an interesting study for a man with the chilled physique of a St. Anthony; for the rest of us she is a maddening problem.

The HILDA was labouring dully, heavily through the broken water, whilst we raced, bobbed, jumped and tore after her.

Malcolm hailed her through the megaphone, and there came back in Carruthers' drawling voice:

"Awfully glad you've come!"

The bowman brought the pinnace dexterously under the HILDA'S port quarter, and Sallie clutched at the yacht's shrouds and sprang aboard. The sub. watched her with frank admiration. Sallie does everything in the open most thoroughly well. I have seen her fall flat on her face at the winning-post in her determination not to be beaten by a longer-legged and swifter opponent. How truly admirable she was, struck us all very vividly as we strove to hoist, pull, and push Dora, aboard. In spite of its æsthetic glory, Dora's figure possesses very obvious limitations in the matter of surmounting obstacles.

Immediately she was on board, Sallie went up to Carruthers and gravely shook hands (Sallie hates being kissed, I speak from careful observation), and drew him aside.

"Jack, until that steam launch is out of sight I'm Miss Crosstrees, daughter of the First Sea Lord. Don't let any of the crew give me away."

"Or the guardship will sink us," I added.

Carruthers looked puzzled, but with a cheery, "all right, Sallie, my bonnie," he went to the side to thank the sub. Carruthers would cheerfully imperil his immortal soul for Sallie. The sub. was brought aboard, and we all drank to the eyes that are brightest, in 1900 Champagne, I have forgotten the brand. The sub. was very obvious, and we all guessed the eyes he pledged— all save Sallie.

As the sub. stood at the side preparatory to descending into the pinnace, Sallie held out her hand, which he took as if it had been some saintly relic.

"I shall always remember your kindness, Mr. — — " (I dare not give his name for fear of the Admiralty censuring him). Then with an arch look added, "I shall tell my father." And the pinnace that had brought a sub. went away with a potential Sea Lord. When the pinnace was about a hundred yards off Dora waved her handkerchief. "Why is it that Dora does these things?" I saw the mute question in Sallie's eyes. The men would have cheered had they dared.

"Carruthers," I remarked as the pinnace sped away from us, "will you put me ashore at once?"

"Why, old man?" he questioned blankly.

"Your most excellent sister," I retorted, "has been posing as the daughter of the First Sea Lord of the Admiralty, without even knowing if he be married or no. I call it disgraceful, and it is likely to produce a pained feeling in Whitehall when it becomes known. That sub. is bound to write to the Admiralty and demand the command of a Super-Dreadnought for his services. I demand to be put ashore at once."

When Carruthers had heard the story he laughed loud and long, and, putting his arm round Sallie, proclaimed hers the best brain in the family.

The log of the Medway guardship would persist in obtruding itself upon my vision. There would be an entry relating to the First Sea Lord's daughter and the service rendered her. The wretched business haunted me. I sought out "Who's Who"; but that gave me no assistance. If the First Sea Lord had a daughter, it might be all right; but if he had not? However, there was nothing to be done but to try to enjoy the trip, and forget the Admiralty.

The HILDA is a 200-ton barge-rigged, sailing yacht, possessed of an auxiliary motor; a boon to the wind or tide-bound yachtsman. Some men affect to despise the aid of a motor, but Carruthers argues that a mariner is not less a mariner because he harnesses to his needs an explosive-engine and a propeller.

Once aboard the HILDA I felt that our adventures were ended. It was perfect weather for idling. The previous day's rain had cleared the heavens of all but a few filmy clouds. There was a good sailing breeze, and the HILDA bent gravely over as she cut through the water on her way seawards. Malcolm was for'ard, lying on his back looking aloft at the swelling canvas. There is no sight so grand or pleasing to a yachtsman's eye as that obtained from this position, and Malcolm knows it. Carruthers was at the helm flirting outrageously with Dora. Sallie was talking with old Jones, the bo'sun and mate, about his latest grandson.

The crew of the HILDA are to a man devoted to Sallie. Tidings that she is to be one of a cruising party means much and self-imposed extra labour, both as regards the HILDA herself and her crew. Everything and everybody are smartened up, and Vincent, the cook, ages perceptibly under the strain of thinking out a menu that shall tempt Sallie to eat. His brow never clears until Sallie has paid him the customary visit of ceremony, which to him is more in the nature of a religious rite.

"Chef"; (she always called him "chef") "it was delicious! Thank you very much indeed," Sallie would say with a grave and gracious smile befitting so great an occasion, a happy, boyish look would spread itself over Vincent's sombre features, and the crew would know that there was to be some dainty at their next meal; for Vincent, when happy, which was extremely seldom, radiated good-will and distributed his largess with unstinting hand.

There is no ecstasy like that of idleness, and no idleness to compare with that felt upon a yacht running before a breeze. Yesterday's troubles are wiped out, and to-morrow's anxieties seem too far off for serious consideration. I was standing musing upon the beauty of the day, watching the HILDA'S track which seemed to trail off into infinity, when I became conscious that the little streak of grey smoke that I had been gazing at for some time came from the funnels of a destroyer, which was evidently being pushed. She was fetching us back to her at a rare pace, and was obviously heading our way. For some minutes I continued idly to watch her. Suddenly the old misgiving assailed me.

Sallie's deception had been discovered, and the irate captain of the guardship had sent to demand an explanation. I strolled over to Carruthers and told him my fears. He grinned with obvious enjoyment. Carruthers is imperturbable. He looked over his shoulder at the destroyer. After a time he called to Sallie, who was sitting amidships, musing.

"They're coming to fetch you, Sallie," he said cheerfully, and then explained his fears. "Shall we fight for you, my girl, or calmly give you up?"

Sallie clapped her hands with glee. To be chased by a warship was a novelty she enjoyed to its fullest extent.

"Will they fire, do you think?" she enquired of Malcolm, trembling with eagerness.

"They'll probably megaphone us to come up into the wind," responded the practical Malcolm.

Sallie's face fell. I really believe she half hoped that the destroyer would endeavour to sink the HILDA. By this time everyone aboard had become conscious that something unusual was happening. The crew stood grouped amidships, talking in undertones and casting side-glances at our little party standing round the wheel. It was now apparent to all that we were the destroyer's objective. On she came like a mad thing, her grey snout tearing at the waters and throwing them over her humped-up shoulders. She looked like some wicked gnome bent on the ruin of the inoffensive HILDA. Sallie's eyes danced with glee. She had never seen anything so magnificent as this sinister creature that came bounding towards us. We all watched breathlessly. Presently a crisp, metallic voice sounded through the megaphone:

"Yacht ahoy! we want to board you."

A few sharp words from Carruthers and we flew hither and thither, and soon the HILDA with mains'l and tops'l brailed came up into the wind. It was all quietly and prettily done, and our nimbleness much impressed the destroyer's crew, as we afterwards learned.

The destroyer was soon beside us. We expected another megaphone message; but no, they were lowering a boat. Dora became anxious and asked, could we not hide Sallie? Nothing short of extreme physical force could have hidden Sallie at that moment.

The destroyer's boat was soon under our lee, and an officer with the stripes of a lieutenant-commander sprang aboard and saluted Dora and Sallie. The HILDA'S crew stood gazing at us in undisguised amazement. What was going to happen?

Sallie stepped forward.

The officer looked round as if seeking someone.

"Can I speak to Miss Crosstrees?" he enquired, looking from one to the other.

"I am Miss Crosstrees," said Sallie stepping forward.

A look of bewilderment spread itself over the young man's face. Then, as if with sudden inspiration, he plunged his hand into his waistcoat pocket and withdrew a small gold pencil case and held it out to Sallie.

"I think you dropped this in the pinnace. The captain of the guardship— er— er— sent me after you with it." The poor fellow seemed covered with confusion.

"Thank you," Sallie said, as she looked up at him with great, grave, but smiling eyes and with that damnable demureness that sends men mad about her, "but it isn't mine. I didn't drop anything in the launch. Thank you so much," she smiled. "It is so kind of Captain — — . Will you thank him for taking so much trouble?" Then after a moment's pause she added, "No; I will write," and beckoning me to follow she descended to the cabin, where she wrote two blazing indiscretions, one to the Captain of the guardship and the other to the sublieutenant who had taken us off to the HILDA. I strove to prevent her: I remonstrated, I expostulated, I implored; but to no purpose. All I was there for, it appeared, was to tell her that a launch was not a pinnace, to post her as to other technicalities and to do the spelling. When we returned on deck the L.-C. was drinking champagne, whilst the crew of the destroyer's boat drank a mute toast in grog. In their pockets they had already stowed away a handful of Carruthers' cigars.

With much goodwill the boat put off, was hoisted aboard the destroyer, which swung round and, with a valedictory moan from her syren, darted off home again bearing important despatches from Sallie to the Captain of the Medway guardship and one of his junior officers.

"What did you say in that note?" I enquired of Sallie, visions of a prosecution for forgery flitting through my mind.

"Oh, I just thanked him," said Sallie nonchalantly; but I saw by the dancing lights in her eyes that there was something else.

"And— — ?" I interrogated.

"Oh! I told him the truth and asked him to come to tea and bring that nice boy who had helped us."

"Sallie," I remarked severely, "captains of battleships do not generally take their junior officers out to tea."

But Sallie only smiled.

Later the cause of the young officer's confusion was explained in a letter he wrote to Sallie. He was engaged to Miss Crosstrees.

There was an unusual silence at the conclusion of the story, unbroken even by Bindle's mallet. Bindle insisted on a mallet upon being elected as chairman. It was obvious that Sallie had cast her spell over the Night Club.

"I'd a-liked to 'ave been one o' them officers. A real sport 'im wot didn't give 'er away," remarked Bindle at length meditatively. Then turning to me he enquired:

"Don't yer think, sir, we ought to sort o' revise them rules about ladies? We didn't ought to be narrow-minded."

"He's got Sallyitis," laughed Carruthers.

"Yes, I got it bad, sir," flashed Bindle, "an' I want a smile from 'er wot give it to me."

"What about your views on hens?" enquired Dare.

"Well, sir," replied Bindle with quiet self-possession, "a single little 'en won't do us any 'arm."

And that is how it came about that Sallie Carruthers was unanimously elected a member of the Night Club.

I doubt if anything ever gave Sallie greater pleasure than this tribute, particularly as she was always treated as one of ourselves, except by Angell Herald, who could never forget that he was something of a "ladies' man."

CHAPTER III
THE PRIME MINISTER DECIDES TO ADVERTISE

One of the characteristics of the Night Club is its mixed membership.

"Rummy crowd, ain't we?" Bindle had remarked to Sallie Carruthers the first night she was present. "There ain't a pair anywheres, except p'raps you an' me, miss."

And so it was, the only thing we have in common is our humanity. To see Angell Herald doing the "ladies' man" to Sallie is a sight that gives the rest of us a peculiar joy.

"'E do work 'ard, an' she bears it like a good un," was Bindle's comment.

Angell Herald's views on women are those of the BON VIVEUR of the saloon bar. When he addresses Sallie his whole manner changes, just as most people's idiom undergoes revision when they write a letter. You can see the dear fellow pulling himself together and, metaphorically, shooting out his cuffs and straightening his tie as a preliminary to opening fire. His manners are superb, elaborate, suburban. If Sallie happen to wander near the door, Angell Herald dashes forward and opens it, attracting general attention and arresting everybody's conversation.

"He's got more manners than breeding," Dare once whispered to me after a particularly elaborate demonstration of Herald's politeness. If Sallie rises, Herald comes to his feet with a suddenness that has been known to overset his chair.

He has no humour, but many jokes— most of which are for men only. It took him some time to gauge his company, when Dick Little introduced him to our circle, and it came about thus.

One evening he had told a particularly pointless "man's story," and his was the only laugh that announced its conclusion. Dick Little strove to smooth over the hiatus; but Bindle, whose disgust was obvious, had thrown a bomb upon troubled waters by enquiring of Dick Little with great innocence, "Let me see, sir, I think you said you was out o' carbolic'!" From that date Angell Herald's stories were merely pointless without being obscene. Sallie's presence was a good influence.

In spite of his limitations, Angell Herald is not a bad fellow, and he told us many amusing stories of the "publicity" world. He knows Fleet Street thoroughly from the "box-office" point of view, and he seems to regard the editorial aspect of the newspaper world with amused tolerance. "Where would those scribblers be," he would enquire with fine scorn, "without adverts.? Yet would you believe it," he had once said to Dare, "they look down upon us?"

"Most extraordinary," Dare had responded.

"Still it's a fact," Angell Herald had assured him, with the air of a man who knows from a friend at the Admiralty that fifty German submarines were sunk during the previous week.

Angell Herald was always the publicity agent, even when telling his stories. Dare had once said with great truth, "There is more herald than angel about the dear chap."

Dare was particularly interested in the following story:—
The morning had begun badly. The coffee was cold and the bacon burnt. Angell Herald spoke to Mrs. Wiggins about it, and she had promptly given notice. In Mrs. Wiggins it was nothing new for her to give notice. She generally did so twice a week; but this was the third time during the current week, and it was only Tuesday. Angell Herald had been forced to apologise. He hated apologising— except to a client. Then there was an east wind blowing He disliked east winds intensely, they affected his liver.

On the way to the office he called in and had his hat ironed. He also bought a rose. He always buys a rose when there is an east wind, and he likewise always has his hat ironed; it mitigates the pinched expression of his features.

As he entered his office, he was conscious of not replying to Pearl's "Good morning." Pearl is Angell Herald's clerk, the only member of his staff. With somewhat ambiguous humour Angell Herald calls him "the pearl of great price," as every fortnight with painful regularity he asks for a rise— he never gets it. When Pearl is not asking for a rise, he is soliciting a half-holiday in which either to marry a friend, or bury a relative. Pearl is entirely lacking in originality. That is what makes him a most admirable clerk for an advertising man.

On this particular morning, Angell Herald each had a funeral on the same day. They closed the office and met at Epsom! Neither referred to the matter subsequently.

On this particular morning Angell Herald saw that Pearl was in a state of suppressed excitement. Something had happened. Was it another friend desirous of getting married, or a double death? Pearl himself, however, settled the matter by saying:

"There's a letter from No. 110 Downing Street, sir."

Then, of course, his employer knew that it was merely insanity.

"Don't be an ass, Pearl," was the retort. Angell Herald allows Pearl a considerable amount of licence, because he is valuable to him. Furthermore, he permits his subordinate to joke sometimes, in lieu of increasing his salary.

Pearl's reply was to produce a letter, franked with the stamp of the Prime Minister. Angell Herald tore it open, hurriedly, and read:—
To Angell Herald, Esq.,

382 Fleet Street, E.G.

DEAR SIR,

Your name has been given to me as an expert in the matter of publicity. I shall be glad if you will call here at 10.30 to-morrow with regard to a matter of considerable importance.

I am,

Yours faithfully,
A.   LLEWELLYN JOHN.

Angell Herald was overwhelmed. Mr. Llewellyn John, who had held office for years with the Waightensea Ministry, and had just formed a Government of his own, was sending for him, Angell Herald, Publicity Agent, and furthermore had signed the letter himself. It was bewildering. What could it mean?

Angell Herald, turning to Pearl and, pulling himself together, announced casually:

"I shall probably be some time, Pearl. I have an engagement with"— and he mouthed the words— "Mr. Llewellyn John, at Downing Street, at 10.30, which will probably occupy me some time."

The burnt bacon, the cold coffee, Mrs. Wiggins' notice; all were forgotten in the dropping of Pearl's jaw. It was a delight to his chief to see the clerk's surprise.

At 10.25 sharp, Angell Herald was enquiring for Mr. Llewellyn John at 110 Downing Street. It was clear that he was expected. He was led along a corridor, through a wide hall, and eventually into a large room. From the further corner a little man, with generous grey hair or a more than conventional length and a smile of bewildering sunniness, rose and came towards him.

"Mr. Angell Herald?" he enquired.

Angell Herald bowed. He had momentarily lost the power of speech. The Prime Minister held out his hand, Angell Herald grasped it. He was prepared to grasp anything to make up for his silence.

"Pray, sit down," said the Prime Minister. "I want to have a confidential chat with you."

Angell Herald sat down. He twirled his hat in his hands. He was conscious of the perfume of his rose, and that he was behaving like an ass. He looked round the room. He felt he could do anything in the world save look at this great little man, who sat smiling opposite to him. It was Mr. Llewellyn John who broke the silence.

"Now, Mr. Herald. I hear you are an expert of publicity methods."

Angell Herald bowed.

"You may be wondering why I sent for you?"

Angell Herald muttered something to the effect that he was.

"Well," said the Prime Minister deliberately, "it is because I have decided to advertise."

"To what, sir?" blurted out the astonished publicity agent.

"To advertise. Why should not a Government be advertised just as a pill, a concert-singer, or a rubber-tyre? Everybody advertises, and we must advertise. Those who don't will go to the wall— or in Opposition, which is the same thing."

Angell Herald introduced a tactful little laugh. It was a success.

"Certainly," he replied, beginning to feel more at ease. "Quite naturally, I agree with you. Now, an inspired article, for instance, in THE AGE, an illustrated interview in THE BRITON, with pictures of yourself playing with dogs, children and things, a— — "

"My dear sir, those are obsolete methods. We are living in a new age, an age that requires novelty. If you advertise in the right way, you will get your public; but you have to hit it very hard to make it look. My friend Mr. Chappledale, for instance, he advertises; but there is no originality in his methods. Sir Lomas Tipton, he advertises; but how? I might endeavour to get together a football team to 'lift' the English Cup; but what good would that do?"

"Quite so," was the dazed response, "quite so."

"Take the late Lord Range, for instance," continued Mr. Llewellyn John. "He understood modern methods. Instead of stating, as some antiquated Minister might, that the King and country needed 300,000 high-explosive shells, he said: 'Lord Range calls for 300,000 high-explosive shells.' He was up to date, and he got them. A magnificent fellow Range. Didn't care a— ahem! for anybody. Was even rude to me," he muttered reminiscently. "I liked him for it.

"Now take the Cyrils, that famous Parliamentary family dating back for centuries. They do not know how to advertise. Ten years hence there won't be a Cyril in the House of Commons. There may be a few in the House of Lords— that depends on democracy.

"Then there's my old friend Waightensea. He did not advertise as the needs of the political situation demanded he should, and the result is that he has had to go. It does not matter who you are in these days— bishop or blacksmith, Prime Minister or pierrot— you've got to advertise— the war has brought us this!"

Hitherto Angell Herald had regarded himself as second to none in the advertising world; but Mr. Llewellyn John made him feel a child at the game.

"The most far-seeing man in Europe has been the Kaiser. He was the first who understood the true value of advertisement, and he ran it for all he was worth. We laughed at him, but we listened. Some people think he overdid it a little," this with a smile; "but still among monarchs he certainly was the first to appreciate that you have got to run a monarchy rather as you have a patent medicine, spend ninety per cent. of your money on advertising, and the other ten per cent. on the article itself— less if possible."

Again the Prime Minister flashed upon his visitor that bewildering smile. Angell Herald hinted that this would be a very big business, involving many thousands of pounds.

"Quite so," remarked Mr. Llewellyn John. "Now, the point is, what can this additional expenditure be charged up against? It can't be travelling expenses, because even a Prime Minister could not spend five figures a year on travelling. Secret Service would be difficult. Personally I rather lean to the Naval Estimates."

"The Naval Estimates!" cried Angell Herald.

"Exactly," was the reply. "We are always a little inclined to be penurious over the Army; but if there is one thing that an Englishman is generous about— always excepting the question of meals— it is the Naval Estimates. Yes," he continued, as if to himself, "I think we might charge it up against the Naval Estimates.

"It is of no use making speeches, no one reads them. We don't care for politics. We are a nation of grumblers in search of scapegoats. As you know, I broke into epigrammatic utterances. Look at their success. You will remember what a sensation I created with that clarion call of mine, 'Now we sha'n't be long!' the cables and Marconi installations thrilled and stuttered it throughout the habitable globe. I followed it with "Arf a mo',' which was even more popular. My greatest cry, however, was 'Pip-pip!' which has been translated into two hundred and eighty-seven languages and dialects."

Angell Herald smiled sympathetically. He had never felt so much like a schoolboy undergoing instruction than as he listened to this remarkable man, who was teaching him his own business.

"And now, for the future," continued Mr. Llewellyn John, "we are going to strike out a new line. I intend to advertise my Ministry, advertise it as no ministry has ever been advertised before. I will make the Kaiser look parochial and Mr. Moosephalt provincial. Now let us get down to brass tacks. America is wonderfully apt in her expressions. I only discovered this after she joined the Allies. Have you a notebook with you, Mr. Herald?"

"Yes, sir," replied Angell Herald, hastily drawing one from his pocket, relieved at having something to do.

"Now listen," the Prime Minister continued. "I propose to have pages in the principal newspapers devoted to separate subjects. One will be, for instance, 'The Home Life of England.' There will be pictures of myself and family enjoying the home life, entertaining my friends at home, golfing, playing hop-scotch with my children— — "

"But," interrupted Angell Herald, "isn't the Home Life stunt a little played out?"

"Exactly, my dear Mr. Herald, exactly. That is just what I was coming to. There will also be pictures showing me entertaining guests at the Ritz-Carlton, at the Opera, at the pantomime, at the theatre, at the races, at Westminster Abbey, at boxing matches."

"But," interrupted Angell Herald, "how is this to be called 'The Home Life?'"

"My dear sir, the Larger Home Life, the Larger Home Life. Get that well into your mind. I am appealing to the great public, not the relics of the early Victorian Era, the Little Home-Lifers, sitting one on either side of silly artistic fireplaces, gaping into each other's stupid eyes, and looking and feeling unutterably bored. Let us have the Large Home-Lifers. Occasionally, when the weather is warm, I shall put in an appearance at the public swimming-baths; my figure will stand it."

"Excellent!" Angell Herald murmured. "Wonderful!" He was thrilled by this man's genius.

"Then another would be 'The Fleet'— Great Britain's Love for Her Navy.' It's a fine call, it's a thrilling call. I shall have myself photographed entering the train, lunching in the train, getting out of the train, being received by the local authorities. Then I shall see myself pictured with Sir Goliath Maggie on board THE ALUMINIUM EARL. I shall make a speech about the Nelson touch, dragging in the CHESAPEAKE and SHANNON, and touching lightly upon the story of the REVENGE. No, on second thoughts I cannot do that. America has come in, and Spain may at any moment. No," he added musingly, "that will not do. They say I lack statesmanship, and that would give them an admirable peg. No, we'll let that go."

"Then again I shall deal with the Woman Question, from a new point of view. I shall speak more or less sympathetically upon the subject of revolutionary propaganda and sedition. Here I shall bring in another famous epigram I have prepared. 'The Hand that rocks the Empire rules the World.' I shall be photographed receiving flowers, having my hat knocked off by an irate woman, possibly being embraced by another woman in a moment of political ecstasy. That will appeal to the public tremendously."

"Excellent!" murmured the bewildered publicity agent, conscious of the inadequacy of the word.

"But there is one important thing. To each of these huge scale advertisements there must be a moral. There must be something that will appeal to the imagination of the Briton, and, as you and I know, nothing so appeals to him as that which touches his pocket. It is Democracy that will rule the world in future. Now in the case of the Home Life of England, for instance, I shall comment upon the unnecessary extravagance that I have observed in certain quarters, notably the gorgeous uniforms of the officials at the Ritz-Carlton. I shall pass a Bill quickly through the House taxing silk stockings for men and the wearing of calves. That will please the public.

"Then with regard to the Navy, I shall call attention to the enormous amount of brass-work. I shall incidentally refer to the fact that something like a quarter of a million per annum is spent on brass-polish for the Navy. I shall give the necessary orders through the First Lord that all brass-work shall in future be japanned, and so on."

"Mr. Llewellyn John," Angell Herald burst out, "what a loss you are to the advertising world!"

The Prime Minister smiled, and continued:

"Then there comes the personal question. There must be little paragraphs about myself constantly in the papers. For instance, as I am leaving this place I slip in getting into my car, and have to be led back into the house. There will be photographs of the policeman who rushes up, the look of solicitude on his face. There will also be photographs of the policeman's wife and the policeman's daughter— possibly a son or nephew serving at the front. My family will be photographed at the windows, looking out anxiously to see what has happened. There can also be a few personal particulars about my chauffeur.

"Later I shall be photographed limping out of the house and being helped into the car by three secretaries, four policemen and my chauffeur. In the press there will be comments upon my stoicism. How, in spite of being in obvious pain, I put the affairs of the Empire before those of my own person. Later, possibly there may be an attempt to abduct my daughter. Another time there can be an attempt on my life."

"On your life, sir?"

"Oh, yes, yes," he continued airily. "These things can always be arranged. You see, I can be walking in some lonely place, and you can come up and— well, knock me down."

"Me!" gasped Angell Herald in ungrammatical horror.

"Exactly," he replied, as if it were the most ordinary thing in the world for a publicity-agent to knock down a Prime Minister. "A great sensation would be created, and it would extend to the ends of the earth. We could suggest that the Kaiser was deeply involved in the plot.

"Again, I can slip on a banana skin, and run a shirt Bill through the House providing that everyone who eats bananas must carry about the skins until he gets home, where they must be put in the dust-bin. This would gain for me the vote of every human being who has ever slipped on a banana skin.

"Finally we come to the epigrammatic phrases. There is one I have in mind that should create a sensation. It is: 'One of these days you'll see what you won't wait for.' I got it from one of the furniture men who assisted when I moved into No. 110; a droll fellow, an exceedingly droll fellow. His name was— let me see, yes, Joseph Bindle. I thought of asking him to join my Ministry, but I remembered the prejudice that one has to fight in this country in all matters affecting innovation. Another phrase that may be useful to us is: 'All is not cult that kulturs.'

"Oh! by the way, couldn't we run 'The Twenty-three Gentlemen who are always too late' on the lines of 'Ten Little Nigger Boys?' I think there's something in that.

"But we must first have some refreshment. Ah! here it is."

A maid entered with a tray on which were two glasses of milk and three small oatmeal biscuits. Angell Herald took the milk, but refused the biscuits. Mr. Llewellyn John took the other glass and a biscuit, which he put on the table beside him. When the maid had retired he explained with a laugh:

"My official lunch, the photographer and cinema operator will be here in a minute. We expect great things from both the photograph and the film. 'An Ascetic Premier' we are calling it. Now drink your milk."

Angell Herald gulped down a mouthful of the unaccustomed fluid, and put down the glass well out of reach.

"Yes," continued Mr. Llewellyn John, "there is a vast field before us. Now, Mr. Herald, will you or will you not throw yourself wholeheartedly into this project? It is a chance of a lifetime. Will you become the first Head of my Publicity Bureau? You can name your own terms. I want you to do the thing thoroughly, and no expense will be spared."

For some reason or other Angell Herald found himself dumb. He could do nothing but gaze at Mr. Llewellyn John in bewilderment. He strove to speak. His tongue seemed to cleave to the roof of his mouth. Mr. Llewellyn John looked at him in surprise.

"Do you hear me, sir? Do you hear me, sir?" he vociferated, banging his hand on the table. "Do you hear me, sir?"

Then something seemed to happen. The scene faded, and Angell Herald found that it was not Mr. Llewellyn John's voice, but that of Mrs. Wiggins; and he was in bed, and somebody was knocking outside his door, obviously Mrs. Wiggins.

"Do you hear me, sir?" she repeated. "It is eight o'clock, and I've knocked three times."

"An' you dreamt all that, sir?" enquired Bindle of Angell Herald.

"Every word of it," Herald replied as if scorning to lay claim to imagination.

"Wonderful!" was all Bindle said, and the eye that looked over the brim of his pewter caught mine and the lid slowly drooped and then raised itself again. There is a world of expression in Bindle's eyes— when taken singly.

The story had really been a "rag" planned by Dick Little and Dare, whom Angell Herald had told that he dreamed he had been asked by Mr. Llewellyn John to become Minister of Publicity, and we had looked forward with some interest to see how he would take the yarn. He had accepted it, without comment.

"That chap would accept anything that he thought increased his own importance," said Carruthers after Angell Herald's departure.

"Fancy them a-knowin' all about me at Downin' Street," remarked Bindle as he rose to go.

CHAPTER IV
THE BOY

The "Assassins," as Carruthers called Tims' men, were all-powerful at the Night Club. They were always in sufficient strength to form a majority; but in reality Bindle exercised a sort of unconscious despotism. When a question arose, we instinctively looked to Bindle, who in turn looked to Sallie.

"When I first 'eard that frogs come out o' tadpoles, I couldn't 'ardly believe it," Bindle once remarked, "but when I looks at the Assassins an' remembers that they'll become doctors in top 'ats, with a you-leave-it-to-me-an'-I'll-save-yer-if-I-can look, well, after that I'll believe anythink."

"What's the matter with us?" enquired Roger Blint, a little dark man with a quiet manner and a violent soul.

"Well, as far as I can see, there ain't nothink wrong wi yer as men; but doctors— !" Bindle shook his head despondently. "I wouldn't trust my young life to one of yer."

Bindle fixed his gaze on Jim Colman, the recognised leader of all demonstrations, physical and vocal. Colman has the instincts of a mob-leader, but the most delicate "touch" among the younger men at Tims. He is destined for Harley Street and a baronetcy.

"Look at Mr. Colman," continued Bindle. "'Ow'd jer like to 'ave 'im 'oldin' yer 'and an' tellin' yer to get ready for an 'arp?"

"Well, what about Bill?" enquired Colman. "He looks harmless enough— what?"

Bill Simmonds is a little sandy fellow, with a bald, conical head, who beams upon the world through gold-rimmed spectacles, which give him a genial, benevolent expression. He looks for all the world like "a clever egg," as Dare once described him.

"Well," remarked Bindle, judicially, examining Bill Simmonds' face, "I might be prepared to trust 'im wi' my soul; but as for my body, well, give me Mr. Dennett or Mr. Smith. I'm like Mrs. B.; I like 'em big."

Hugh Dennett is an international three-quarter who has made football history, whereas Archie Smith was the amateur champion heavy-weight when the war broke out.

"I ain't got anythink to say against you as sports," said Bindle encouragingly; "but as doctors, well, well!" And again he shook his head with mournful conviction.

Tims' men never talk "shop," but from scraps of conversation among themselves that I have overheard, theirs is a strenuous life. Sometimes they do not see their beds for three consecutive nights; yet they are always cheery and regard whatever they have to do as their "bit." One complaint they have, that they are not allowed to go to the front.

All seem to find in the Night Club relaxation from strenuous days and sleepless nights. According to Bindle, who is a recognised authority upon such matters, they are a cheer-o! crowd. It was they who had been loudest in their support of Sallie's election, and when "the Boy's" story came to be told, they were equally definite in their view that he must be invited to join our exclusive circle. These were the only two instances of stories told at the Night Club resulting in our membership being increased. Incidentally the Boy fell in love with Sallie, and this formed an additional bond of sympathy between him and us.

I

To his brother officers he was always "The Boy." The men, with more directness of speech, referred to him as "The Kid," whilst at Whitehall he was known as Second Lieut. Richard St. John Custance Summers, of the 8th Service Battalion Westshire Regiment.

How he managed to secure his commission no one ever knew.

"Must 'a been 'is bloomin' smile," was the opinion of the platoon sergeant, expressed to the company-sergeant-major. "The men make fools o' theirselves about the Kid."

Chubby-faced, languid of manner, forgetful and "frightfully sorry" afterwards, even in his khaki he did not look more than sixteen. At mess he sat as if he had collapsed from sheer lack of bone necessary to keep him rigid. He literally lolled through life.

In carrying out his duties, such as he was unsuccessful in evading, he gave the impression of being willing in spirit, but finding great difficulty in getting his body to respond to his wishes.

One day the Colonel, a big blue-eyed man, whom the men called "the Kid's nurse," had told him that he had "the spirit of a martinet, but the body of a defaulter," which was not a bad description for the C.O., who did not incline to epigram.

When given an order, the Boy would salute, with that irresistible smile of his that got him out of some scrapes and into others, then off he would lounge, all legs and arms, like a young colt, although as a matter of fact he was below medium height. When he made a mistake the N.C.O.'s and men contrived to correct it, with the result that his was the smartest platoon in the battalion. The Senior Major had once said to him:

"Boy, you're the slackest young cub I've ever met, yet you get more out of the men than the Colonel and I combined. How is it?"

"I suppose, sir," replied the Boy with great seriousness, "they see I'm such an awful ass that they're sorry for me."

The Boy got more leave and took more leave than any other officer in the division, and no one seemed to resent it. He never did anything in quite the same way as another youngster would, and he was a constant source of interest to his brother officers.

One roystering night he had returned to his quarters in a state ill-befitting "an officer and a gentleman," and the company-sergeant-major, aided by a corporal, had put him to bed and they had mutually sworn eternal secrecy. In the morning, although the two non-coms. had managed to convey to him that only they knew of the episode, the Boy had gone to the Colonel, and before the other officers said:

"I returned to barracks last night drunk, sir. I was very drunk and I think I was singing. I'm sorry. It sha'n't occur again."

The Colonel asked who had seen him, and on being told that only the company-sergeant-major and a corporal knew of the incident, he burst out with:

"Then why the devil do you tell me about it?"

"I wanted you to know, sir. It was rather rotten of me. I know you hate it, sir, and it's a bad example."

The C.O. turned aside to hide a smile. The idea of the Boy being an example to anyone or anything amused him; but being a disciplinarian, and understanding something of the Boy's nature, he stopped a week-end leave due some ten days hence, and from the Boy's smile as he saluted he saw that he had done the right thing.

One day the Boy was given charge of his company in a sham fight, at which as everybody knew the Brigadier was to be present.

With his command, the Boy was like a kitten with a skein of wool. He got it hopelessly tangled. Perspiring and swearing N.C.O.'s strove in vain to evolve order and find out exactly where they were.

Suddenly, with a yell to fix bayonets and charge, the Boy darted forward followed by the men in a manner that would have broken the heart of a drill-sergeant. They had blundered upon an enemy field battery in the act of limbering up, and the Boy returned to camp with six guns and a stream of prisoners, and the Brigadier had spoken to the Colonel of the exploit.

"Talk about luck! Blimey! That Kid'll save the bloomin' regiment one o' these days," grinned a private, as the boy marched with rather a bored air at the head of his day's bag.

The Boy continued to avoid as if by instinct all the duties he possibly could. Indeed, he was apparently aided and abetted by officers and men alike. When at last the word arrived to prepare to entrain for an unknown destination, the Boy's chief concern had been about his kit. The C.O.'s instructions had been definite and incisively expressed. He ordered that nothing be taken that was not absolutely necessary, and had added that he did not want to see France lumbered up with cast-off articles of kit of the 8th Westshires.

There had been rather a heated argument between the Boy and his captain as to the interpretation of the word "necessaries."

"My boot-trees and manicure set," said the Boy, "are as necessary to me as your trousers are to you."

"Rot!" the captain had replied. "You'll be thinking more of your skin than of your nails when you get out there."

The Boy had compromised by leaving the boot-trees and taking a pocket manicure set.

In the trenches he was the same imperturbable, languid half boy, half man he had been in England. He was as indifferent to shells and bullets as to the grins of the men as he lolled against the parados polishing his nails. Sometimes he would bewail the lost boot-trees as he surveyed his hopeless-looking foot-gear.

At first the uncleanliness of trench life had roused him from his accustomed languor, but later he accepted this and what it entailed, not with philosophic calm, but because protest involved effort.

Even when towards the end of the September that culminated in Loos it became known that the 8th Westshires were to take part in "the big push," and whilst officers and men were eagerly discussing their chances, he remained his sunny, imperturbable self.

On the night before the charge, the Colonel had sent for him to go to his dug-out, and there had told him that early in the morning he was to go back with an important message to Divisional headquarters and await a reply, which he was to bring back after the action. Without a word the Boy gave the necessary acknowledgment and saluted, but there was a mutinous look in his eyes as he wheeled round and left the Colonel's dug-out.

He spoke to no one, although many of his brother officers watched him to see how he would take it. The C.O. had conferred with the Senior Major, and decided that he could not risk the Boy's life, a view that was entirely endorsed by every officer and man in the regiment.

For hours the Boy stood brooding and polishing his nails. Then, just before "stand-to" he disappeared. His captain was the first to discover the fact, and enquiry was made along the whole line of trenches, but no one had seen the Boy for at least half an hour.

II

The guns had opened their brazen throats in a frenzy of hate. Overhead shells whistled and hissed, lumbered and howled as they tore towards the enemy trenches, a hurricane of screaming hate. Gusts of shrapnel spat death from above, and rifle and machine-gun bullets buried themselves impotently in the sandbags amid little puffs of dust. Slowly dawn shivered into day— a day of greyness and of death.

In the assembly-trench the 8th Westshires were waiting. Heavy-eyed and silent they gazed towards the enemy lines, hidden by a curtain of dense yellow smoke. Against the parapet scaling ladders were placed ready. At a word, a short snapping sound barked along the trench, the ladders suddenly became alive, as men scrambled up and passed over the top, or fell backward with a dull thud.

"No rushing, a steady advance in open order," had been the Colonel's last words to his officers.

The 8th Westshires formed up and, as steady as on parade, advanced. They had not proceeded more than thirty yards when with a sigh a breeze swept past them and carried the yellow gas beyond the first enemy trench, like a curtain of fairy gauze.

Machine-guns and rifles poured a merciless fire into the Westshires. Everywhere men were dropping, silently or with little coughs of surprise. They advanced a further twenty yards and then faltered. With a shout the Colonel dashed on waving his stock. The moment of uncertainty seemed to pass, when suddenly the Colonel dropped.

"My God!" muttered the Senior Major, as he saw the indecision pass like a wave along the line; he also noticed several men had turned and were stealing back to the trenches they had just left. "They'll— they'll— — " and there was a sob in his voice.

Just at the moment when retreat seemed inevitable, a figure rose from a small shell-crater, and with a yell that no one heard waved on the Westshires.

"It's the Boy," gasped an officer. "Where the hell— — "

"It's the bloomin' Kid. Well I'm damned!" roared the colour sergeant. "'Ere, come on, or they'll nab 'im."

This was enough for the Westshires. Capture the Kid? Not if they knew it. With a howl they raced for the enemy trench, overtaking the Boy two yards from the sand-bags. The men's blood was up. They tumbled into the first trench, and with a sickening "sog sog" their bayonets got to work. Little coughs and grunts told of men doubled up. Everywhere cries of "Kamerad" were heard.

"It's no use yellin', sonny," one man was heard to say. "You've got to 'ave it— you've go to 'ave it!" and he drove his bayonet into a German's massive loins.

The Boy had come through untouched. Like a moth he flitted about from place to place, and wherever he was, there the fighting would be at its fiercest. Not only had the second line of trenches been taken in accordance with instructions, but the Westshires had crushed all resistance in the first, which they should have left to a following battalion. The work done, the Boy called two stretcher-bearers, and went back in search of the Colonel.

III

That night the Colonel sat in a German dugout, with a heavily bandaged leg. He had refused to go to the rear. He must first see the Boy.

When he entered, the Boy saluted and stood as if waiting for something that he knew would happen, but in which he was not particularly interested.

"What have you to say?" the Colonel enquired with unsmiling eyes. In the 8th Westshires officers and men alike dreaded the absence of that smile which seemed so much a part of the Colonel's eyes.

The Boy hung his head. "I'm sorry, sir," he said, in a low, husky voice.

"You remember my orders?"

"Yes, sir."

"Yet you absented yourself without leave."

"It was— — " the Boy stopped; his voice seemed suddenly to forsake him. Then after a moment's pause the words came in a rush.

"It was the old dad, sir. I've never let him know I'm such a rotter. If he knew I was sent to rear before the charge it would have crocked him. He— he— thinks no end of me."

The Boy stopped again and looked at the Colonel. "I crept out this morning, and lay in a small crater near our trench until the advance.

I was going to join up and I thought I should get killed. He would sooner have me dead than not there. I'm sorry, sir— I'm— — " The Boy's voice trailed off into a sob.

"You know what you did to-day?" enquired the Colonel. The smile was back in his eyes, but the Boy did not see it.

"Deserted!" The word came out with a jerk.

"Yes, you deserted— that is, technically— but you saved the whole battalion from being cut up and— possibly disgraced."

The Boy looked at the C.O. in wonder. He blinked his eyes uncertainly.

"I— I don't— — "

"Listen, Boy! You were sent out by my orders on listening-patrol, and told to join up with the Battalion when it advanced. You did so, do you understand?"

"But listening-patrols aren't sent out under bombardment, sir."

"Damn you, Boy, what the devil do you mean? Am I C.O. or you?" The Colonel wanted to laugh and simulated anger to preserve his authority.

"I'm sorry, sir; but— — "

"Well, never mind about listening-patrol. I shall send an account of your services to the General that will get you the D.S.O., possibly the V.C. I will write to the— er— old dad myself." The Colonel's voice was husky.

"Now, get out, Boy, damn it— get out at once!"

And the Boy got out.

There was the vigour of conviction in Bindle's play with his mallet, and the hum of talk at the conclusion of the story made it obvious that the Boy had considerably enlarged the circle of his friends.

"He's a dear!" Sallie blinked her eyes vigorously. They were suspiciously moist.

"'Ere, 'ere, miss," agreed Bindle. As a matter of fact Bindle always agrees with anything that Sallie says.

"I say, Windover, couldn't you bring him round one night?" enquired Dick Little.

"I'll try," said Windover. "He's stationed at Wimbledon now."

"And did he get the V.C.?" enquired the practical-minded Angell Herald.

"No, the D.S.O.," replied Windover, "with promotion to a first lieutenancy."

"What a shame," said Sallie, and turning to Windover she said, "You will bring him, Winnie, won't you?" Sallie and Windover are old friends.

And that is how the Boy became a "Night-Clubber." He is a strange combination of impudence and innocence; but there is one way of bringing him to heel. It was quite by accident that I discovered it.

One evening he had been roasting poor Angell Herald rather badly, and although that astute person was sublimely unaware of what was taking place, both Dick Little and I thought things had gone far enough.

I happened to have with me the manuscript of the story of how the Boy got his D.S.O. Without a word I started reading from it in a loud voice. I had not got six lines down the page before he slowly dragged himself out of the armchair in which he was lounging, his face crimson, and, walking towards the door, remarked:

"You'll find me on the mat when you've done reading rot."

That is the Boy all over.

CHAPTER V
THE BARABBAS CLUB

I have some acquaintance with authors; but of all I have encountered Jocelyn Dare is in many ways the most remarkable. Careless, generous, passionate, he is never so happy as when narrating the enormities of publishers. His white, delicate fingers will move nervously, his long black locks fall over his alabaster forehead, and his black eyes flash as he describes the doings of these "parasites" and "pariahs," as he calls them.

He is a thoroughly good fellow in spite of this eccentricity, never withholding a helping hand from anyone. I believe he would succour even a publisher if he found one in need of help; but he can no more resist denouncing the fraternity than he can keep the flood of raven hair from falling over his eyes when he becomes excited.

Bindle likes him, and that is a testimonial. They have something in common, as Dare's heart, like Bindle's "various" veins, is a bar to his doing his bit, and Dare feels it as much as does Bindle.

"I like to listen to Mr. Gawd Blast 'ammerin' tacks into publishers," Bindle would remark appreciatively. "An' don't 'e know some words too!"

Dare's vocabulary is almost unique. He is a master of the English tongue. At rhetorical invective I have never heard his equal, and I have encountered a Thames lighterman in one of his inspired moments. Bindle would sit in mute admiration, watching Dare as he flung the mantle of obloquy over "that cancer polluting the face of God's fair earth."*

*To those who are not authors it should be explained that Dare refers to publishers as a whole.

It was Dare who told us the story of the author who, unable to extract his royalties from a publisher, seized him by the beard and swore he would hang on until the money was forthcoming. "And that," he concluded, "is why not one publisher in a hundred wears a beard."

It was Dare, too, who told us of the author who went to a certain well-known publisher with a manuscript, saying, "My previous books have been published by— (and he mentioned the names of three honoured firms)— and they were rogues to a man, did me right and left, only I could never catch them, not even with the help of the Society of Authors. So I've brought my new book to you, Mr. Blank."

The publisher was delighted at the compliment and, smiling in his most winning manner, enquired, "And may I ask why you come to me, sir?"

He waited expectantly, his lips still bearing the after-glow of the smile.

"I come to you, Mr. Blank," the author replied impressively, "because you are an honest man."

And the publisher fainted.

Dare would laugh with the joyousness of a schoolboy when telling these yarns. But there is no malice in him. He is as mischievous as a puppy; but as soft-hearted as a woman.

There is something strangely lovable about Dare. Certain of his mannerisms are in themselves feminine; yet he is never effeminate. One of these mannerisms is what might be called the fugitive touch, which is with a woman a caress. He will lay his hand upon your coatsleeve just for a second, or put it across your shoulders, a slight brushing movement, which betokens comradeship.

He adores children. I have seen him, when exquisitely turned out in top hat and morning coat, pick up a howling youngster that had come a cropper, brush it down, stay its cries and stop its tears, and send it home wreathed in rainbow smiles, clutching a generous-sized bag of sweets. Such is Jocelyn Dare.

When the time came for a story, he told that of the Barabbas Club. For some time I hesitated to write it up for the Night Club. I regarded it as too limited in its appeal. At last, however, I decided to let the Club judge for itself. Dare took great interest in the writing of the story, and himself read and corrected the typescript.

I

"My dear fellow," said Jocelyn Dare, "the Seven-headed Beast of the Apocalypse is nothing to it. It's absolutely unique."

With the air of a man who has completed a life's work, Dare tapped some sheets of manuscript that lay upon the table, selected a cigarette from the box with a care and deliberation usually bestowed upon cigars, and proceeded: "You are a doctor, whose mission in life is to purge and purify the human body; I am a novelist whose purpose it is to perform the same office for the human soul."

From the depths of a particularly comfortable easy-chair, Dick Little looked up good-humouredly at his friend.

"You're a queer devil, Dare. One of these days you'll get a shock— poseurs always do."

Dare laughed easily, and Dick Little continued. "But what have publishers to do with the human soul? That's what puzzles me."

"There is only one thing, my poor Little," replied Dare, looking down at the other with a smile of pity, "that makes friendship between you and me at all possible."

"And that is?"

"Your incomparable understanding of my corpus, which you persist in calling my liver. I give you all credit for this. You know my constitution to a nicety, and in a way you are responsible for my novels."

"Good God!" ejaculated Dick Little, sitting up in his chair with an expression of alarm upon his features. "I hope not."

"Listen!" said Dare. "A publisher is an obstacle to intellectual progress. He is a parasite, battening upon the flower of genius. That is why we founded the Barabbas Club. It frankly encourages authors to quarrel with their publishers. No one is eligible for membership who cannot prove conclusively to the Committee that he has been extremely rude to at least one publisher. I myself have been grossly insulting to seventeen different publishers, on several occasions before their own clerks. I have taken three into Court— I confess I lost each case— and I horsewhipped him who published THE GREATER PURITY because he failed to advertise it sufficiently."

"And what happened?" queried Dick Little, who had heard the story a score of times.

"I was summonsed for assault. The magistrate was a creature entirely devoid of literary perception. He fined me five guineas, plus five guineas damages, and two guineas costs. But wait! Now here comes the shameful part of the story. Later I discovered that I had been wrong about the advertising. I wrote to that worm, that foul weed who is poisoning the slopes of Parnassus, apologising for whipping him, and will you believe it, he absolutely refused to return the five guineas damages?"

Dick Little laughed. He always laughed to see Dare upon his hobby-horse.

"The result of that case was an addition to the rules of the Barabbas Club, by which it was provided that, whenever an author horsewhipped a publisher, with or without justification, the president of the club should resign, and his place be automatically filled by the horsewhipper."

Dick Little rose from his chair, stretched himself lazily, lighted another cigarette and prepared to take his departure.

"One moment, my dear fellow," remarked Dare, "I must tell you something about this, THE DAMNING OF A SOUL." He tapped the manuscript upon the table. "It gives a picture of a publisher, so vivid, so horrible, so convincing, that I shudder when I think that anything so vile can be permitted to exist by our most gracious sovereign lady, Nature. It tells of the gradual intellectual murder of a great genius through lack of proper advertising by his publisher. 'It is a masterly picture of the effect of advertising matter upon imaginative mind.' I quote the words of our President. It will create a sensation."

"But what about libel?" enquired Dick Little, whose more cautious nature saw in this same masterpiece a considerable danger to its author.

"There is my master-stroke. My Beast, which transcends that of the Apocalypse in horror-compelling reality, is, as was that, a composite creature. I have drawn upon the whole of the seventeen publishers with whom I have had differences. One supplies 'a nervous, deceitful cough,' another 'an overbearing manner,' a third 'a peculiar habit of crossing and recrossing his legs,' a fourth 'a swindling propensity when the day of reckoning arrives,' a fifth 'a thoroughly unclean and lascivious life,' a sixth 'a filthy habit of spitting into the fireplace from every conceivable angle of his room,' a seventh— — "

"Enough! I must be off," laughed Dick Little. "I suppose it's all right; but one of these days you'll get yourself into a bit of a mess. There may be the devil to pay over this even."

Dare smiled indulgently as he shook hands.

"Good-bye, my Æsculapius," he said. "If there's trouble, I have behind me the whole of the members of the Barabbas Club, representing eight hundred and thirteen volumes, and the brains of the country. Good-bye." There was a note of weariness about Dare's voice. Materialism was exceedingly tedious.

"Well, it's his affair, not mine," muttered Dick Little to himself as he descended the stairs of Dare's flat; "but they don't fight with books in the King's Bench Division."

II

Three weeks later, on returning from a fortnight's holiday in Scotland, Dick Little found awaiting him at his chambers the following note from Dare:—

"Come round at once. There is not the Devil, but the publishers to pay. Bring a hypodermic syringe and a pint of morphia.— "J.D."

Dick Little had been out of the world, and he had forgotten all about THE DAMNING OF A SOUL and his own misgivings. Having seen a few of his more important patients, he walked round to his friend's flat and found Dare in a pathetic state of gloom.

"Have you brought the hypodermic syringe and the morphia?" he asked without troubling to greet his visitor.

"What! Tired of life?" questioned Dick Little smiling.

"I am tired of a civilization that is rotten, and which makes injustice possible."

"What has happened?"

"I published THE DAMNING OF A SOUL in THE CORMORANT, and arranged with the editor for a copy to be sent to every publisher in the country. Ye gods!" and Dare laughed mirthlessly.

"And what happened!" asked Dick Little.

"Twenty-five writs for libel up to date," groaned Dare, "and God knows how many more to come."

Dick Little laughed loud and long.

"How many publishers went to the making of your Beast of Parnassus?" he asked.

"Only seventeen; that's the peculiarly damnable part of it.

"And what do they say at THE CORMORANT?"

"Well, I've kept away from the offices, where all the writs have been served by the way, and I've written a formal protest to the Postmaster-General against the use of the telephone for language that is entirely unfit for even the smoking-room of a woman's club. NOW they write; but as I don't read the letters, it doesn't matter so much."

"The editor is in a passion, I suppose?"

"No; he's in a nursing-home. He's a master of diplomacy," replied Dare wearily. "I'd do the same, only I can't afford the fees. It's the general-manager who telephones. I'm going to put him in my next novel, curse him!"

"In addition to a writ," Dare proceeded, "each publisher has written me a letter, 'without prejudice' and with considerable heat."

"What about?" enquired Dick Little, thoroughly interested in the curious situation that had arisen out of Dare's unfortunate story.

"The man who crosses and recrosses his legs says that he is the only publisher in the world with that characteristic, and that I accuse him of unclean morals, as if a publisher had any morals, clean or otherwise. He of the nervous cough objects to the adjective 'deceitful,' and is having his books examined by an accountant He who salivates into the fireplace from impossible angles, is producing the testimony of three specialists to prove that he has chronic bronchitis, and that it is neither infectious nor contagious, and so on." Dare's voice trailed off drearily.

"And what do you propose to do?" questioned Dick Little.

"Do?" enquired the other, listlessly throwing himself into a chair and lighting a cigarette. "Do? Why, nothing. That's why I want the morphia. I'm the imperfect, not the present tense. I'm done."

"How about the Barabbas Club?" asked Dick Little.

"Dissolved."

Dick Little whistled.

"Dissolved," continued Dare, "because its work is accomplished, vide the Presidential valediction. I don't see how; but it's too tedious to bother about."

Dick Little went to the sideboard and poured out some water into a glass, then emptying into it the contents of a small phial that he took from his pocket, returned to where Dare sat and bade him drink.

"What is it— a death potion?" enquired Dare lazily as he swallowed the dose.

"Wait and see!" replied the other.

For a quarter of an hour they smoked in silence. Suddenly Dare bounded into the air, and rushed to the telephone.

"Piccadilly 1320, quickly," he shouted. Then a minute later, "That THE CORMORANT? I want the general-manager. Yes; it's me. Oh, shut up! I've got a plan. Coming round. Three more writs? Wish it were thirty. We'll do 'em yet— 'bye."

Snatching up his hat and entirely oblivious of his friend's presence, Dare rushed out of the room; and a moment later the bang of the front door told that he had left the flat.

"Never saw strychnine act so before," muttered Dick Little as he picked up his hat and gloves and prepared to go.

III

Ten days later as Dick Little sat in the consulting-room of his surgery, waiting for seven o'clock to strike that the first patient might be admitted, Jocelyn Dare burst through the door followed by the protesting parlour-maid.

"Sorry, old man; but I had to tell you. We've won. It's a triumph for Letters, and all due to your science and my brain. As I said before, your understanding of my corpus is incomparable."

"It's five minutes to seven," remarked Dick Little evenly, "and the first patient enters at seven."

"Of course. Well, three minutes will suffice. I found a scapegoat."

"A what?"

"A scapegoat. You see if I could prove that my publisher was some particular person, we should have only one action to defend; but if that publisher were dead, and we could square his relatives, then we were safe.

"I set about discovering a dead publisher, and you would be astonished to find how rare they are. They seem to be immortal, like their asinine brothers. At last I lighted upon Sylvester Mylton, who died a bankrupt nearly a year ago. By great good luck I ran his wife to earth. She was in terrible straits, almost starving, poor woman."

"But what— — "

"Wait a moment. I showed her the article, and told her that I felt that I had done a dishonourable thing in writing about the dead as I had done, and would she accept five pounds as compensation. Heavens! I don't think the money pleased her so much as the knowledge that the iniquitous Mylton had been pilloried. He had made her life a curse."

"So far so good. I had to remind her of a few of his characteristics; but she's a shrewd woman, and hunger you know. Now read this." Dare held out a copy of the current issue of THE CORMORANT, pointing to a page bordered by the portraits of thirty publishers. Within the pictorial frame appeared the following:—

THIRTY WRITS FOR LIBEL

AN EXTRAORDINARY OCCURRENCE

A SENSITIVE PROFESSION

"Three weeks ago we published a story from the brilliant pen of Mr. Jocelyn Dare entitled THE DAMNING OF A SOUL, in which was given a vivid picture of an unscrupulous, immoral, gross, and dishonest publisher— a man capable of any vileness, who had by under-advertising the work of a promising young author, damned him for ever. Soon after the appearance of our issue containing Mr. Dare's contribution, writs began to rain in upon us until there was scarcely a publisher in London who had not instructed his solicitors to proceed against us for criminal libel, as, in our picture of the unscrupulous publisher, he thought he saw himself depicted.

"Although we fully recognise the obligations of the living towards the dead, we are, in self-defence, forced to publish a letter that we have received from the wife of the late Sylvester Mylton, the well-known publisher, who died some months ago. It runs:—

"'DEAR SIR,

"'I have read with deep pain and regret the story in your issue of the 2nd inst., entitled THE DAMNING OF A SOUL. In the character of the publisher I recognise my late husband. None can mistake 'the overbearing manner,' 'that peculiar habit of crossing and recrossing his legs,' 'the nervous, deceitful cough,' 'the habit of spitting into the fireplace from every conceivable angle of his room,' although I must add that his accuracy was astonishing. With regard to the other points, I can only say that of recent years I declined to live with him because of the creatures with whom he associated— I do not refer to his authors. I regret that you should have brought him so prominently before the public, and I hope you will send me ten or a dozen copies of your issue containing the story.

"'I am,

"'Yours sincerely,

"'ARABELLA MYLTON.'

"We can only express regret that so many publishers should have thought our story referred to them. We thought that Mr. Dare had painted so vile and heartless a wretch as to prevent any self-respecting publisher from seeing in such a creature any resemblance to himself. Apparently not. Surely Mecænas is the most sensitive of beings. We may add that we shall defend each of the actions threatened. We embellish this page with portraits of the publishers who have caused us be served with writs."

Dick Little read the page with astonishment.

"By heavens! what a score," he shouted. "And the writs?"

"All withdrawn, and the Barabbas Club has regathered and is dining me at the Ritz tonight. God knows who'll pay the bill. I must be off to dress."

And that evening Dick Little thought more of the sensibilities of publishers and the brains of authors than the ailments of his patients.

"Fancy publishers bein' as bad as that," remarked Bindle reflectively, as he took a long pull at his tankard. "They seem to beat foremen."

"Publishers," said Dare, "are pompous asses. If they were business men— if they were only men-of-letters, I would embrace them."

"P'raps that's why they ain't," suggested Bindle.

Dare joined in the laugh against himself.

"I have known some publishers," remarked Angell Herald with characteristic literalness, "who have been most excellent advertisers. I fear Mr. Dare is rather prejudiced."

"Shut up, Herald," broke in Dick Little, "you're thinking 'shop.'"

"P'raps they've got 'various' veins* in their legs, or else their missusses 'ave got religion," suggested Bindle. "It ain't fair to judge no man till you seen 'is missus, an' a doctor's seen 'is legs— beggin' your pardon, miss," this to Sallie.

*Bindle has been repeatedly refused for the Army on account of varicose veins in his legs, and he shows a tendency to regard this affliction as at the root of all evil.

CHAPTER VII
FAIL THE NIGHT CLUB

One evening I failed the Club badly. During the previous week there had not been a moment in which to complete the half-written story intended for that particular Sunday. I had done my best; but I arrived at Chelsea with the knowledge that I had let them all down.

When I had made my confession, Bindle turned to me with grave reproach in his eyes.

"I'm surprised at you, sir," he said, "I been lookin' forward all the week to this evenin', an' now you tell us you ain't got nothink. Wot we goin' to do?"

My unpopularity was sufficiently obvious to penetrate the thickest of skins.

"What about bridge?" ventured Tom Little. But Bindle was opposed to every suggestion made. It was clear that he was greatly disappointed, and he seemed to find solace nowhere, not even in his tankard of ale.

"You done the dirty on us to-night, sir," he said during a pause in the fusillade of personalities and rather feeble suggestions as to how thee evening should be spent. "Sort o' thing a foreman 'ud do."

It was Jocelyn Dare who came to the rescue. "What," he asked, "can you expect of a publisher? He has sufficient manners to impress a half-dipped author, and not enough morals to pay him what is his due."

"My dear Dare," it was Windover who spoke, "are you not inverting the values? Our friend Bindle here, for instance, might reasonably conceive that you place morals on a higher plane than manners. Bindle is young and unsophisticated, you must remember he has arrived at an impressionable age."

Bindle grinned. He scented a battle between Windover and Dare, both brilliant and amusing talkers.

"I'm a Victorian," replied Dare, accepting the challenge with alacrity, "a member of the middle-classes, the acknowledged backbone of the English nation."

"Yes, and like all other respectable backbones should be covered up," retorted Windover.

"Alas!" murmured Dare, gazing at the ceiling. "Once youth was content with Arcadia, now it demands a Burlington Arcadia."

That was characteristic of Dare. An epigram to him justified the most flagrant irrelevancy. Then turning to Windover he added, "But I interrupted you. Let us have your views on morals and manners, or should I say manners and morals?"

"Yes do, sir," broke in Bindle eagerly, "My missus once said I 'adn't no more morals than Pottyfer's wife, I dunno the lady, but p'raps you can 'elp me."

"The association of morals and manners is merely a verbal coincidence," began Windover. "As a matter of fact they exist best apart. Morals are geographical, the result of climate and environment. The morals of Streatham, for instance, are not the morals of Stamboul, although the manners of the one place will pass fairly well in the other. Manners are like English gold, current in all countries: morals, on the other hand, are like French pennies, they must not be circulated in any but the country of their origin."

"Yes; but is this the age of manners or of morals?" asked Dare. "That's what we want to get at."

"Of neither, I regret to say," responded Windover. "We have too many morals at home, and too few manners abroad."

"Excuse me, sir," broke in Bindle, "but wot do you exactly mean by morals an' manners?"

"You are right, Bindle, you invariably are," replied Windover. "Definition should always precede disquisition." He proceeded to light a cigarette, obviously with a view to gaining time. "Observing this rule," he continued, "I will define morals as originally an ethical conception of man's duty towards his neighbour's wife: they are now in use merely as a standard by which we measure failure." Windover paused and gazed meditatively at the end of his cigarette.

"And manners?" I queried.

"Oh! manners," he replied lightly, "are a thin gauze with which we have clothed primæval man and primitive woman."

"But why," enquired Sallie, leaning forward eagerly, "why should the primitive and primæval require covering?"

It was Dare who answered Sallie's question. "Mark Twain said, 'Be good; but you'll be lonely,'" he observed. "Man probably found it impossible to be good, being gregarious by instinct. He saw that Nature was always endeavouring to get him involved in difficulties with morals, and like the detective of romance, determined to adopt a disguise. He therefore invented manners."

"I will not venture to question Dare's brilliant hypothesis," continued Windover. "With the aid of good manners a man may do anything, and a woman quite a lot of things otherwise denied her. It is manners not morals that make a society. Manners will open for you all doors; but morals only the gates of heaven."

"As a eugenist I am with you, Windover," said Dare; "because both manners and eugenics are the study of good breeding."

"Excuse me, sir," broke in Bindle, "but do yer think yer could use a few words wot I've 'eard before? I'd sort o' feel more at 'ome like."

There was a laugh at Windover's expense, and a promise from him to Bindle to correct his phraseology.

"Morals," continued Windover, "are merely the currency of deferred payment— you will reap in another world."

"That's wot Mrs. B. says," broke in Bindle; "but wot if she gets disappointed? It 'ud be like goin' dry all the week to 'ave a big lush up on Sunday, an' then findin' the pubs closed."

"Excellent! Bindle," said Windover, "you prove conclusively that the future is for the proletariat."

"Fancy me a-provin' all that," said Bindle with unaccustomed dryness.

"Morality," continued Windover with a smile, "is merely post-dated self-indulgence. There is a tendency to expect too much from the other world. Think of the tragedy of the elderly spinster who apparently regulated her life upon a misreading of a devotional work. She denied herself all the joys of this world in anticipation of the great immorality to come."

"That's jest like Mrs. B.," remarked Bindle, "Outside a tin o' salmon, an' maybe an egg for 'er tea, there ain't much wot 'olds 'er among what she calls the joys o' mammon."

"Mrs. Bindle," said Windover, picking out another cigarette from the box and tapping it meditatively, "is in all probability intense. Most moral people are intense. They either have missions or help to support them. They wear ugly and sombre clothing adorned with crewel-work stoles. They frequently subsist entirely upon vegetables and cereals, they live in garden-cities and praise God for it— — "

"I, too, praise God that they should live there," broke in Dare.

"Exactly, my dear Dare, probably the only approval that providence ever receives from you is of a negative order."

"You forget the heroes and heroines of morals, Windover," said Dare gently. "Penelope, Lucrece, Clarissa Harlowe, Sir Galahad."

"Manners, too, have had as doughty champions," was the reply, "for instance, the Good Samaritan, Lord Chesterfield, and the wedding guest in THE ANCIENT MARINER. Manners are social and public, whilst morals are national and private. All attractive people have good manners, whereas— well there were the Queen of Sheba, Byron and Dr. Crippen."

Bindle looked from Windover to Dare, hopelessly bewildered. He refrained from interrupting, however.

"Our morals affect so few," continued Windover, "whereas our manners react upon the whole fabric of society. A man may be a most notorious evil-liver, and yet pass among his fellows without inconveniencing them; on the other hand, if he be a noisy eater he will render himself obnoxious to hundreds. Manners are for the rose-bed of life, morals for the deathbed of repentance."

"All this is very pretty verbal pyrotechnics," said Dare with a smile; "but you forget that the greatness of England is due to her moral fibre. I grant you that morality is very ugly, and its exponents dour of look and rough of speech, still it is the foundation of the country's greatness."

"There you are wrong," was Windover's retort, "it is not her morality that has made for this country's greatness, but her moral standard, coupled with the determination of her far-seeing people not to allow it to interfere with their individual pleasures. They decided that theirs should be a standard by which to measure failure. The result of this has been to earn for us in Europe the reputation of being a dour and godly people, who regard the flesh and the devil through a stained-glass window. They forget that to preserve the purity of his home life, the Englishman invented the continental excursion."

"But what about puritan America?" broke in Dare. "If we are smug, they are superlative in their smugness."

"You forget, Dare," said Windover reproachfully, "that they have their 'unwritten law,' said to be the only really popular law in the country, with which to punish moral lapses. To explain the punishment, they created 'brain storm'; but it cannot compare with our incomparable moral standard. It is England's greatest inheritance."

Windover paused to light the cigarette with which he had been toying. It was obvious that he was enjoying himself. Bindle seized the moment in which to break in upon the duologue.

"I don't rightly understand all the things wot you been sayin', you bein' rather given to usin' fancy words; but it reminds me o' Charlie Dunn."

Bindle paused. He has a strong sense of the dramatic.

"J.B.," said Dare, "we demand the story of Charlie Dunn."

'Well, sir, 'im an' 'is missus couldn't 'it it off no 'ow, so Charlie thought it might make matters better if they took a lodger. 'E thought it might save 'em jawin' each other so much. One day Charlie's missus nips off wi' the lodger, and poor ole Charlie goes round a-vowin' 'is life was ruined, an' sayin' wot 'e'd do to Mr. Lodger when 'e caught 'im.

"'But,' ses I, 'you ought to be glad, Charlie.'

"'So I am,' says 'e in a whisper like; 'but if I let on, it wouldn't be respectable, see? Come an' 'ave a drink.'"

"There you are," said Windover, "the poison of appearances has penetrated to the working-classes. To the blind all things are pure."

I reminded Windover that Colonel Charters said that he would not give one fig for virtue, but he would cheerfully give £10,000 for a good character.

I could see that Bindle had been waiting to join more actively in the discussion, and my remark gave him his opportunity.

"A character," he remarked oracularly, "depends on 'oos givin' it. I s'pose I taken an' lost more jobs than any other cove in my line, yet I never 'ad a character in my life, good or bad.

"Now, if you was to ask 'Earty, 'e'd say I ain't got no manners; an' Mrs. B. 'ud say I ain't got no morals, an' why?" Bindle looked round the room with a grin of challenge on his face. "'Cause I says wot I thinks to 'Earty, an' 'e don't like it, an' I talks about babies before young gals, an' Mrs. Bindle thinks it ain't decent.

"As I ain't got neither manners or morals, I ought to be able to judge like between 'em. Now look at 'Earty, 'e's as moral as a swan, though 'e ain't as pretty, an' why?"

Again Bindle looked round the circle.

"'Cause 'e's afraid!" Having made this statement Bindle proceeded to light his pipe. This concluded in silence, he continued:

"'E's afraid o' bein' disgraced in this world and roasted in the next. You should see the way 'e looks at them young women in the choir. If 'Earty was an 'Un on the loose, well— — " Bindle buried his face in his tankard.

"'Is Lordship 'as been sayin' a lot o' clever things to-night; but 'e don't believe a word of 'em."

Windover screwed his glass into his eye and gazed at Bindle with interest.

"'E loves to 'ear 'imself talk, same as me."

Windover joined the laugh at his own expense.

"'E talks with 'is tongue, not from 'is 'eart, same as 'Earty forgives. A man ain't goin' to feel better 'cause 'e's always doin' wot other people ses 'e ought to do, while 'e wants to do somethink else. If a man's got a rotten 'eart, a silver tongue ain't goin' to 'elp 'im to get to 'eaven."

Bindle was unusually serious that night, and it was evident that he, at least, was speaking from his heart.

After a pause he continued, "My mate, Bill Peters, got an allotment to grow vegetables, at least such vegetables as the slugs didn't want. Bill turns up in the evenin's, arter 'is job was done, wi' spade an' 'oe an' rake. But every time 'e got to work on 'is allotment, a goat came for 'im from a back yard near by. Bill ain't a coward, and there used to be a rare ole fight; but the goat was as wily as a foreman, an' Bill always got the worst of it. 'E'd wait till Bill wasn't lookin', and then 'e'd charge from be'ind, an' it sort o' got on Bill's nerves.

"At last Bill 'eard that 'is allotment was where the goat fed, an', bein' a sport, 'e said it wasn't fair to turn Billy out, so 'e give up the allotment and 'is missus 'll 'ave to buy 'er vegetables same as before." Bindle paused to let the moral of his tale soak in.

"But what has that to do with morals and manners, J.B.?" asked Dick Little, determined that Bindle should expound his little allegory.

"For Bill read England and for goat read niggers," said one of Tims' men.

"You got it, sir," said Bindle approvingly. "As I told 'Earty last week, it ain't convincin' when yer starts squirtin' lead with a machine-gun a-tellin' the poor devils wot stops the bullets that there's a dove a-comin'. Them niggers get a sort of idea that maybe the dove's missed the train."

"Talkin' of goats— — " began Angell Herald.

"We wasn't talkin' o' goats," remarked Bindle quietly, "we was talkin' o' Gawd."

Whereat Angell Herald at first looked nonplussed and finally laughed!

CHAPTER VII
A SURPRISE BEHIND THE VEIL

Windover, or to give him his full name, the Hon. Anthony Charles (afterwards Lord) Windover, apart from possessing a charming personality, has a delightfully epigrammatic turn of speech. It was he who said that a man begins life with ideals about his mother; but ends it with convictions about his wife. On that occasion Bindle had left his seat and, solemnly walking over to Windover, had shaken him warmly by the hand, returning to his chair again without a word.

It was Windover, too, who had once striven to justify celibacy for men by saying that a benedict lived in a fool's paradise; a bachelor in some other fool's paradise.

Windover's meeting with Bindle was most dramatic. Immediately on entering the room with Carruthers, Windover's eye caught sight of Bindle seated at his small table, the customary large tankard of ale before him, blowing clouds of smoke from his short pipe. Windover had stopped dead and, screwing his glass into the corner of his left eye, a habit of his, gazed fixedly at him who later became our chairman. We were all feeling a little embarrassed, all save Bindle, who returned the gaze with a grin of unconcern. It was he who broke the tension by remarking to Windover.

"You don't 'appen to 'ave a nut about yer, do you sir?"

Windover had laughed and the two shook hands heartily, Windover perhaps a little ashamed of having shown such obvious surprise. As a rule his face is a mask.

"I'm awfully sorry, I was trying to remember where we had met," he said rather lamely.

"'Ush, sir, 'ush!" said Bindle looking round him apprehensively, then in a loud whisper, "It was in Brixton, sir. You was pinched 'alf an 'our after me."

From that time Bindle and Windover became the best of friends.

When, on the death of his elder brother, killed in a bombing-raid, Windover had succeeded to the title, we were all at a loss how to express our sympathy. He is not a man with whom it is easy to condole. He and his brother had been almost inseparables, and both had joined the army immediately on the outbreak of war.

On the Sunday following the tragedy, Windover turned up as usual. He greeted us in his customary manner, and no one liked to say anything about his loss. Bindle, however, seems to possess a genius for solving difficult problems. As he shook hands with Windover he said, "I won't call yer m'lord jest yet, sir, it'll only sort o' remind yer."

I saw Bindle wince at the grip Windover gave him. Later in the evening Windover remarked to Carruthers, "J.B. always makes me feel exotic," and we knew he was referring to Bindle's way of expressing sympathy at his bereavement.

Curiously enough, to the end of the chapter Bindle continued to address Windover as "sir", possibly as a protest against Angell Herald's inveterate "my lordliness."

Windover's story was just Windover and nobody else, and it is printed just as he narrated it, with injunctions "not to add or omit, lengthen or shorten a single garment." I have not done so.

How long I had been dead I could not conjecture. I remembered buying a newspaper of the old man who stands at the corner of Piccadilly Place. I recollected that it was my intention to justify, to the smallest possible extent compatible with my instinctive sense of delicacy, the letter of patient optimism that I had received that morning from my tailor. That was all. There had been no death-bed scene, with its pathos of farewells, no Rogers moaning piteously about his future, as he invariably did when my health showed the least deviation from the normal. Yet here was I dead— dead as Free Silver.

In a dingy apartment of four garishly papered walls, upon a straight-backed, black oak settle, I sat gazing into my top hat. That I was dressed for calling did not seem to cause me any very great surprise, nor was I conscious of any tremor, or feeling of diffidence as to my fate. It seemed much as if I were waiting to see my solicitor upon some unimportant matter of business. I knew that I was there to be interrogated as to my past life. I was vaguely conscious that awkward questions would be asked, and that the utmost tact and diplomacy would be required to answer or evade them.

I was speculating as to the probable cause of my death, weighing the claims of a taxi, the end of the world and a bomb, when the door opposite to me opened and a tall angular woman appeared. Given a dusty crape bonnet, she would have passed admirably for a Bayswater caretaker. I was taken aback: in my mind post-mortem interrogation had always been associated with the male sex.

Marvelling that this unattractive Vestal should be an attribute to Eternity, I rose and bowed. My imagination had always pictured the women of the Hereafter as draped in long, white, clinging garments, and possessed of beautiful fluffy wings and a gaze of ineffable love and wonder. The thought of the surprise in store for the sentimental ballad-writers induced a chuckle!

With a gesture of her lean hand, the Vestal motioned me from the room. At the extreme end of a gloomy corridor along which we passed, there appeared a grained door bearing in letters of white the words:—

MRS. GRUNDY

PRIVATE

My interest immediately became stimulated. Here was an entirely unlooked-for development.

"Shall we go in?" I enquired, rather out of a spirit of bravado than anything else.

The Vestal rebuked me with an expressionless stare. Presently the door opened with a startling suddenness and later closed behind us of its own accord.

The second room seemed strangely familiar. On the mantel-piece was a large gilt clock in a glass case, flanked on either side by an enormous pink lustre with its abominable crystal drops. The furniture was either ponderous or "what-notty", and every possible thing was covered, as if to be undraped were indelicate. On the chairs were antimacassars, table-cloths hid the shameless polish of the wood, the pattern of the Brussels carpet was modified in its flamboyancy by innumerable mats. The walls were a mass of pictures, and in front of the only window were lace curtains of a tint known technically as "ecru." There were two collections of impossible wax fruits covered by oval glasses, a square case of incredibly active-looking stuffed birds, and a bewildering mass of photographs in frames. Here and there on tables were a few select volumes, ostentatiously laid open with silk hand-painted bookmarks threading through their virgin pages. I identified "The Lady of the Lake," Smiles, "Self Help," "Holy Living and Holy Dying," the works of Martin Tupper, and the inevitable family bible.

At a large round-table opposite to the door sat a presence— a woman in form, in clothing, in everything but sex. It was quizzing Disapproval in black silk, with a gold chain round its neck from which hung a large cameo locket. Its grey hair, very thin on top, was stowed away in a net with appalling precision. It had three chins, and grey eyes, behind which lurked neither soul nor emotion. It was the personification of the triumph of virtue untempted.

I bowed. The eyes regarded me impassively, then turned to the massive volume before them. It was bound in embossed black leather with gilt edges and a heavy gilt clasp. I was incredulous that the Sins of Society could be all contained in one book; but decided that it was made possible by the use of the word "ditto." Society is never original in anything, least of all its sinning.

In the hope of attracting to myself the attention hitherto considered my due, I began to fidget. Presently, and without looking up, Mrs. Grundy, as I judged her to be, demanded in a smooth, colourless voice:—

"Your name?"

"Anthony Charles Windover," I responded glibly.

"Age?"

I coughed deprecatingly.

"Age?" It was as if I heard the uninflected accents of Destiny.

"Is it absolutely necessary?" I queried.

"Absolutely!"

"Forty-three. Of course in confidence," I added hastily.

"There is no confidence in Eternity."

"Then you, too, are a sceptic?" I ventured. She merely stared at me fixedly, then proceeded to turn over the leaves of the tome in front of her. Soon she found what appeared to be the correct page. After fully a minute's deliberate contemplation of the entry, she looked up suddenly and regarded me with a solemn gravity that struck me as grotesque.

"Not a very bad case, let's hope," I put in cheerfully. "There have been— — "

"Silence!"

I started as if shot, and looking round discovered beside me the impassive visage of the ill-favoured Vestal of the ante-room.

"I wish you wouldn't bawl in my ear like that," I snapped. "It's most unpleasant."

"Anthony Charles Windover," it was Mrs. Grundy who spoke in a voice that was deep-throated and disapproving, "age forty-three." She looked up again with her cold and malevolent stare; "yours is a grave record; we will deal with it in detail."

"Surely, Madam," I protested, "it is not necessary to go over everything. I am so hopeless at accounts."

"First there was the case of Cecily Somers," she proceeded unmoved.

"A mere boy and girl affair. Cecily was young, and— well, it didn't last long."

"Then there was the case of Laura Merton," continued the arch-inquisitor.

"Poor Laura," I murmured. "I never could resist red hair, and hers was— — poor Laura!"

"There were circumstances of a very grave nature."

"You mean the curate? He was a bloodless creature; besides it all ended happily."

"You intervened between an affianced man and wife," continued Mrs. Grundy.

"I am very sorry to appear rude, Madam," I protested hotly, irritated by the even, colourless tones of her voice, "but it was Laura's hair that intervened! Am I to blame because she preferred the ripeness of my maturity to the callowness of his inexperience?"

"You caused her mother— an estimable lady— indescribable anguish of soul."

"She hadn't one," I replied, triumphantly, "She was a scheming old— — "

"Silence!" fulminated the Vestal again.

"Really, madam," I protested with asperity, "unless you request this person not to shout in my ear, I shall refuse to remain here another minute."

"There was Rosie de Lisle— — "

"Ah, what ankles! what legs! what— — " I was interrupted by a gurgle from the Vestal in whose eyes there was something more than horror. I turned and found Mrs. Grundy obviously striving to regain the power of speech.

Conscious that my ecstasy upon Rosie's legs had caused the trouble, I hastened to explain that I had seen them in common with the rest of the play-going world.

"Rosie was the belle of the Frivolity," I proceeded, "Bishops have been known to hasten ordinations, or delay confirmations because of Rosie's legs. She danced divinely!"

Rosie's legs seemed to have a remarkable effect upon Mrs. Grundy. She hurriedly turned over the pages of her book and then turned them back again.

"There was Evelyn Relton— — "

"A minx, madam, to adopt the idiom of your sex, whilst my kisses were still warm upon her lips— — " Another gurgle from the Vestal and a "look" from Mrs. Grundy,— "she married a wealthy brewer, and is now the mother of eight embryo brewers, or is it nine?"

"You— you are aggravating your case, stammered Mrs. Grundy, with some asperity.

"I am very sorry, but your attitude annoys me; it always did. I'm a social free-trader, a bohemian— — "

"STOP!" thundered Mrs. Grundy. "That word is never permitted here."

"I think you're extremely suburban," I replied. "You might be Tooting, or even Brixton from your attitude."

Ignoring this, Mrs. Grundy proceeded to read the names of a number of women who had long ceased to be to me anything but names. I could not even remember if they were dark or fair, tall or short. At last she reached Mary Vincent, relict of Josiah Vincent, pork-packer of Chicago.

"Why, she was a most shameless person," I cried. "I am surprised, madam, that you should support such a woman. She actually proposed to me."

"Ahem!" coughed Mrs. Grundy, apparently somewhat taken aback.

"A fact! She asked me if I did not think a middle-aged man— she was always impertinent— would have a better chance of happiness with a woman of ripe experience, a widow for instance, than with some mere inexperienced girl. Really a most offensive suggestion."

"It's very curious," muttered Mrs. Grundy, as she turned over the leaves in obvious embarrassment. "It's very curious, but I see no record here of any such conversation."

"Ha! I thought your books were defective," I exclaimed, now feeling thoroughly at my ease. "Why, I have letters, shameless letters, from Mrs. Vincent, which would make your hair stand on end." I did not appreciate until too late how thin and sparse her hair really was.

"We will proceed," was her response. I was secretly glad that she had dropped that even tone of inevitability and remembered Tully's axiom "make a woman angry and she is half won over."

"There was the case of Sir John Plumtree, 26th baronet. You committed a most brutal assault upon that most distinguished man."

"Plumtree was a bounder, more at home in his own country house than among gentlemen. I certainly did punch his head in the club smoking-room; but do you know why, madam?"

"There is no mention of the cause," said Mrs. Grundy, a little ill at ease.

"We were discussing a very charming member of your sex"— (Mrs. Grundy started and coughed, the word "sex" evidently distressed her)— "when Plum, as we called him, growled out that all women were— I really cannot repeat it, but he quoted a saying of a well-known Eastern potentate whose matrimonial affairs were somewhat— "

"We will pass on," said Mrs. Grundy, huskily. I thought I detected a slight reddening of the sallow cheeks, whilst the Vestal coughed loudly.

"I should really prefer not to pass over this little affair so lightly," I remarked sweetly, seeing my advantage. "There were several circumstances which— "

"We will pass on," was the firm reply, "I will not proceed with that specific charge." The smile with which I greeted this concession did not conduce to put my interlocutor at her ease. "There are certain unconventions recorded against you. We will take a few of the most glaring."

"Why this reticence? Can we not take them all and in chronological order?" I enquired, settling myself in the most comfortless of chairs. Disregarding my request, Mrs. Grundy proceeded:

"On the night of June 7th, 1914, you dined with Mrs. Walker Trevor at — — ," she paused and bent over the register.

"This is very strange," she muttered, SOTTO VOCE. "I don't quite see the reason of this entry. There seems to have been a mistake."

"Can I assist you?" I ventured, becoming interested.

She paid no heed to my offer, and after a few minutes' silence proceeded in the same half-muttering voice.

"Dined with Mrs. Walker Trevor, wife of Captain Walker Trevor, absent on military duty, at Princes, P.R. It does not say what prince, but rank is— — " She paused, then continued: "There is no breach of the conventions in dining at a prince's, even with a married lady whose husband is away. I cannot understand the meaning of P.R. either. It is very strange, very strange indeed."

Here I broke in. "Permit me, madam, to explain. I think you are labouring under a mistake. Princes is a famous Piccadilly Restaurant, which has lost some of its one-time glory through the opening of the Carlton and the Ritz. 'P.R.' of course means Private Room. It was Millicent's idea."

At this juncture there was a loud knocking, evidently at the end of the corridor, followed by expostulations in an angry voice and interjections of "Silence!" in what appeared to be a replica of the Vestal's tones. Mrs. Grundy looked up, scandalised enquiry imprinted on her visage.

"I'm goin' in, I tell you," the angry voice was now just outside. "Get out of the way, you old Jezebel! Silence? I'm damned if I'll be silent. Why I've sneezed three times already. Draughty hole! Get out of the way I say."

The door burst open and there entered a little man in a very great passion. I recognised him instantly as the Duke of Shires, a notorious viveur and director of wild-cat companies. I leant forward and whispered to Mrs. Grundy the name of her illustrious visitor.

"This is an unexpected pleasure, Duke," I remarked smilingly. He regarded me for a few minutes coldly.

"Who the devil are you, and who's that old — — sitting there?"— indicating Mrs. Grundy. Then without waiting for a reply, he continued: "I know you now: you're the feller that said that dashed impertinent thing about my being the Duke of Shares."

"I had the honour, Duke, of immortalising Your Grace in epigram. Wherever the English language is— — "

"Then be damned to you, sir," was the angry response.

"We were not expecting Your Grace yet," interposed Mrs. Grundy; I was astonished at the unctuous tones she adopted in speaking to the Duke.

"No, nor I, confound it! I've just been knocked down by a taxicab, light green, driver had red hair, couldn't see his number."

"I am extremely sorry," croaked Mrs. Grundy in what she evidently intended to be ingratiating tones. "Will not Your Grace take a seat."

"No, I won't!" the Duke tossed his head indignantly. "Draughty hole— damn it, sir, what are you grinning at?"

The remark was directed at me. The little man made a dive in my direction, and in stepping back to avoid him I knocked my head violently against what appeared to be the mantel-piece, although I had been sitting several yards from it.

✻   ✻   ✻   ✻   ✻

"What is it?" I looked about dazed. Two policemen were bending over me, and behind them was a sea of interested faces that looked very pale, I was out of doors, apparently sitting on the pavement, with my head propped up upon a policeman's knee.

"It was a banana skin, sir," responded one of the policemen, holding up something before my eyes— (how the police love an "exhibit")— "you 'urt your 'ead, sir, but you're all right now."

"And Mrs. Grundy and the Duke?" I queried.

"'E re's the stretcher!" said a voice.

"It's a bad business, I'm afraid 'e'll— — "

Then my mind trailed off into darkness and my body was trundled off to St. George's Hospital, from which the almost tearful Rogers later fetched me in a taxi, bemoaning the narrowness, not of my escape from death, but his own from destitution.

"I wonder wot 'Earty 'ud think o' that little yarn," Bindle remarked meditatively as he tapped the table before him with his mallet in token of applause. As chairman Bindle modelled himself upon him who lords it over the public-house "smoker." "'E wouldn't like to 'ave to give up 'is 'arp with angels flapping about."

"But it's only a— a— sort of dream, like mine," interjected Angell Herald, with a touch of superior knowledge in his voice.

Bindle turned and regarded Angell Herald as if he were an object of great interest. Then when he had apparently satisfied himself in every particular about his identity, he remarked quietly with a grin:

"O' course it was. Silly o' me to forget. Poor ole 'Earty. I wouldn't 'ave 'im disappointed. 'E's nuts on 'arps."

CHAPTER VIII
THE MAKING OF A MAN OF GENIUS

It was rather by way of an experiment that I determined to try the effect of irony upon the members of the Night Club. I confess I was curious as to how it would strike Bindle, remembering that remarkable definition of irony as "life reduced to an essence." The story had been told me by Old Archie, if he had another name none of us had ever heard it, who keeps a coffee-stall not far from Sloane Square. He was a rosy-faced little fellow, as nippy as a cat in spite of his seventy years, and as cheerful as a sparrow. He has seen life from many angles, and there has come to him during those three score years and ten a philosophy that seems based on the milk of human kindness.

Had he been gifted with a ready pen, he could have written a book that would have been valuable as well as interesting. "A man shows 'is 'eart an' a woman 'er soul round a coffee-stall," was one of his phrases that has clung to my memory. "Lord bless you, sir," he said on another occasion, "there's good an' bad in everyone. Even in a rotten apple the pips is all right."

I chose a night for Old Archie's story when I knew there would be a full attendance, and without anything in the nature of an introduction began the tale as he had told it to me.

In arriving at a determination to marry, Robert Tidmarsh, as in all things, had been deliberate. It was an act, he told himself, that he owed to the success he had achieved. From the time when he lived with his parents in a depressing tenement house in Boulger Street, Barnsbury, Robert Tidmarsh had been preoccupied with his career. It had become the great fetish of his imagination.

In childhood it had brought down upon him scorn and ridicule. Studious habits were not popular in Boulger Street; but Robert remained resolute in his pursuit of success, He saw that in time the star of his destiny would take him far from Boulger Street— it had. At the age of thirty-eight he was head clerk to Messrs. Middleton, Ratchett & Dolby, Solicitors, of 83 Austin Friars, E.C., wore a silk hat and frock-coat, lived at Streatham, drew a salary of two hundred and thirty pounds a year and had quite a considerable sum in the bank. Boulger Street had been left far behind.

In its way Boulger Street was proud of him; it had seen him mount the ladder step by step. It had made him, nourished him, neglected him, ridiculed him, and later, with the servility of a success-loving plebeian, it respected and worshipped him. He remained its standard by which to measure failure. The one thing it did not do was to imitate him.

Robert saw that, economically, the way was clear before him. His career demanded the sacrifice; for somehow he could never quite rid his mind of the idea that marriage WAS a sacrifice. Such considerations belonged, however, to a much earlier stage of his reasoning. Whatever he had to resign was laid upon the altar of ambition. If destiny demanded sacrifice, he would tender it without hesitation, without complaint.

As he had climbed the ladder of success, Robert found to his surprise that his horizon was enlarging; but he was not deceived into the belief that it would continue to expand to infinity. Being something of a philosopher, he knew that there must be limitations. In a vague, indeterminate way he was conscious that he lacked some quality necessary to his continued progression. He could not have put it into words; but he was conscious that there was something holding him back.

Could he at twenty-one have started where he was at thirty-eight, there might have been a prospect of achieving greatness for the house of Tidmarsh. This he now knew to be impossible, and he wasted no time in vain regrets. His reason told him that, but for some curious shuffling of the cards, he was unlikely to rise much higher. "But should twenty-six years of work and sacrifice be allowed to pass for nothing?" He could not himself climb much higher, but if a son of his were to start from the social and intellectual rung whereon he now stood, there would be a saving of twenty-six years. Then again, his son would have the advantage of his father's culture, position, experience. Slowly the truth dawned upon him; he was destined to play Philip to his son's Alexander. From the moment that Robert Tidmarsh reached this conclusion marriage became inevitable.

For weeks he pondered on the new prospect he saw opening out before him. He was pleased with its novelty. The weakness of the reasoning that a son starts from where his father stands did not appear to strike him. With a new interest and energy he walked through miles of streets adorned with the latest architectural achievements in red brick and stucco. It was characteristic of him that he had fixed upon the avenue that was to receive him, long before his mind turned to the serious problem of finding a suitable partner in his enterprise.

Robert Tidmarsh's views upon women were nebulous. Hitherto girls had been permitted to play no part in his life. He had studiously avoided them. A young man, he had told himself, could not very well nurture a career and nourish a wife at the same time. He was not a woman-hater; he was merely indifferent; the hour had not struck.

For weeks he deliberated upon the kind of wife most likely to further his ends. His first thought had been of a woman of culture, a few years younger than himself. But would the cultures war with one another? The risk was great, too great. He accordingly decided that youth and health were to be the sole requisites in the future Mrs. Tidmarsh.

At this period Robert began to speculate upon his powers of attraction. He would seek to catch a glimpse of himself in the mirrors he passed in the street. He saw a rather sedate, dark-haired man of medium height, with nondescript features and a small black moustache. In a vague way he knew that he was colourless: he lacked half-tones, atmosphere. He studied other men, strove to catch their idiom and inflection, to imitate their bearing and the angle at which they wore their hats. He began to look at women, mentally selecting and rejecting. One night he spoke to a girl in Hyde Park, but he found conversation so difficult that, with a muttered apology about catching a train and a lifting of his hat, he fled. As he hurried away he heard the girl's opinion of him compressed into one word as she turned on her heel, midst a swirl of petticoats, to seek more congenial company. That night he found his philosophy a poor defence against his sensitiveness.

Robert Tidmarsh would have turned away in horror from the suggestion that he depended upon a casual meeting with some girl in Hyde Park to furnish him with a wife. This was intended to be merely an adventure preliminary to the real business of selection. He did not know what to talk about to women, and the knowledge troubled him. When the time came he found, as other men have found, an excellent subject ready to hand— himself.

Robert may be said to have entered seriously upon his quest when he joined a dancing-class, a tennis-club and learned to manage a punt. He afterwards saw that any one of these recreations would have supplied him with all the material he could possibly require. Eventually his choice fell upon Eva Thompson, the daughter of a Tulse Hill chemist. She was pretty, bright, and to all appearance, strong and healthy. He was introduced to the parents, who were much impressed with their potential son-in-law.

Mrs. Thompson was subjected to a dexterous cross-examination, the subtlety of which in no way deceived that astute lady. Accordingly the result was satisfactory to both parties. Eva herself at twenty-two had all the instincts of a February sparrow. To mate well she had been taught was the end and aim of a girl's life, a successful marriage, that is from the worldly point of view, its crown of wild olive. To Robert, however, marriage was the first step towards founding a family. Risks there were, he saw this clearly, but where human forethought could remove them they should be removed.

One of the secrets of Robert's success had been a singleness of purpose that had enabled him to pursue his own way in spite of opposing factors. He was always quietly resolute. It was not so much by his perseverance that he achieved his ends, as by the care which he bestowed upon each detail of his schemes. As in his career, so with his marriage, in itself a part of the scheme of his life. Too astute to be convinced by a mother's prejudiced evidence, or by his own unskilled judgment, he determined to have expert opinion as to Eva's fitness to become the mother of an Alexander. A slight chill the girl had contracted gave him his opportunity. During an evening walk, he took her to his own doctor, who had previously received instructions. Such a thing did not appear to him as callous; he was not marrying for romance, but for a definite and calculated purpose.

To some men marriage is a romance, to others a haven of refuge from rapacious landladies; but to Robert Tidmarsh it was something between a hobby and a career. He asked but one thing from the bargain, and received far more than he would have thought any man justified in expecting. From the hour that he signed the register in the vestry, the training of his son commenced.

Among other things, Robert's reading had taught him that a child's education does not necessarily begin with its birth. Accordingly he set himself to render his bride happy. There was a deep strain of wisdom in this man's mind, which no amount of undigested philosophical reading could quite blot out. He saw the necessity of moulding his wife's unformed character; and he decided that first he must render her happy. He took her to the theatre, with supper at a cheap restaurant afterwards, followed by the inevitable scurry to catch the last train. Occasionally there were week-ends in the country, or by the sea. In short the model son of one suburb became the model husband of another.

Months passed and Robert's anxiety increased. As the critical period approached he became a prey to neurasthenia. He lost his appetite, started at every sound, was incoherent in his speech, and slept so ill as to be almost unfit for the day's work.

There is one night that Robert Tidmarsh will never forget. For two hours he paced Schubert Avenue from end to end, his mind fixed on what was happening in the front bedroom of Eureka Lodge. The biting East wind he did not feel. He was above atmospheric temperatures. His life's work, he felt, was about to be crowned or— — he would not permit himself to give even a moment's thought to the alternative. The suspense was maddening. As he paced the Avenue he strove to think coherently. He strove to compare his own childhood with that which should be the lot of his son. Coherent thought he found impossible. Everything in his mind was chaotic. Had he really any mind at all? Would he lose his reason entirely? Then he fell to wondering what they would do with him if he went mad?

He had got to this point, and had just turned round, when he saw that the front door of Eureka Lodge was open and a woman's figure standing out against the light. With a thumping heart, Robert ran the fifty yards that separated him from the silhouetted figure as he had not run since boyhood. What could it mean— a mishap? As he stopped at the gate, his trembling fingers fumbling with the latch, he heard a voice that seemed to come from no-where telling him that his ambition had been realised. For the first time in his manhood he felt the tears streaming down his face as he clutched at the gate-post sobbing. Fortunately the woman had fled back to her post, and he was spared what to him would have appeared an intolerable humiliation.

During the days immediately following that night of torture, Robert felt that his life was to be crowned indeed. Hitherto the great moment of his career had been when he was called into Mr. Middleton's room, and, in the presence of the other partners, told that he was to be promoted to the position of chief clerk. Now a greater had arrived, and from that hour, when a son was born to the ambitious and self-made solicitor's clerk, his life became one series of great moments.

Robert Tidmarsh early found the rearing of a man child productive of grave anxieties. The slightest deviation from what he considered to be the normal condition of infants produced in him a frenzy of alarm. His forethought had provided books upon the rearing of infants. He consulted them and his fears increased. Convulsions held for him a subtle and petrifying horror. A more than usually robust exhibition of crying on the part of Hector Roland (as the child was christened) invariably produced in his father's mind dismal forebodings. In time, however, he became more controlled, and the arrival of the customary period of measles, whooping-cough, scarlet-fever and other childish ailments found him composed if anxious.

But nervous solicitude for the boy's health did not in the least interfere with the father's dominant preoccupation. The question of education was never wholly absent from his thoughts. With so pronounced a tendency to narrowness, it was strange to find with what wisdom and foresight he entered upon his task. As if by instinct he saw that influence alone could achieve his object. He would form no plan, he would guide, not direct his son's genius. Above all he would not commit the supreme indiscretion of taking anyone into his confidence. Sometimes he was tempted to tell Eva of his ambition, he yearned for sympathy in his great undertaking, but he always triumphed over this weakness.

Eva was a little puzzled at his solicitude about her health, and the frequent cross-questionings to which she was subjected as to what she ate and drank; but woman-like she saw in this only evidence of his devotion. He talked often of children whose lives had been imperilled by injudicious indulgence on the part of their mothers. When the time came for the child to be fed by hand, Robert made the most careful enquiries of the doctor and his father-in-law as to the best and most nutritious infant foods. The result of all this was that the child showed every tendency to become a fine healthy young animal.

But in the care of the body, Robert Tidmarsh by no means neglected the budding mind of his infant son. When the period of toys and picture-books arrived, the same careful discrimination was shown. The old fairy stories, with well-printed illustrations, diverted the young Hector's mind just as the best foods nourished his body. When he tired of literature there were cheap mechanical toys, bought in the hope of stimulating the germ of enquiry as it should manifest itself. People shook their heads and thought such extravagance unwarranted; but Robert smiled. They did not share his secret.

As the years passed and Hector grew up into a sturdy youngster, his father watched furtively for some sign as to the direction that his genius was to take; but Hector, as if desirous of preserving to himself the precious knowledge, refused to evidence any particular tendency beyond a healthy appetite, a robust frame and a general enjoyment of life.

With the selection of Hector's first school, an affair productive of acute anxiety and many misgivings, commenced the education proper of the man-to-be. The first official report, so eagerly awaited, was noncommittal; the second proved little better, and the third seemed to indicate that Hector was by no means an assiduous student. If the boy evinced no marked tendency towards the acquirement of book-learning, he showed an unmistakable liking for out-door sports and stories of adventure. He was encouraged to read the works of "healthy" writers such as Kingston and Ballantyne, strongly recommended by the book-seller who had charge of Robert Tidmarsh's literary conscience. In the winter evenings the boy would pore over the thrilling adventures of the heroes with an attention that did not fail to arouse his father's hopes.

The first tragedy between this Philip and Alexander was the discovery, in the pocket of the younger, of a copy of THE FIREBRAND OF THE PACIFIC; OR THE PIRATE'S OATH, a highly-coloured account of doings of a particularly sanguinary cut-throat. On this occasion Robert Tidmarsh showed something almost akin to genius. He took the book and deliberately read it from cover to cover, subsequently returning it without comment to his nervously-expectant son. The next evening he brought home a copy of THE TREASURE ISLAND, recommended by the bookseller as the finest boy's book ever written, and without a word gave it to Hector. After dinner, the Tidmarshes always "dined," Hector dutifully commenced to read. At nine o'clock his mother's reminder that it was bed-time was received with a pleading look and an appeal for another five minutes, to which Robert signified assent. At ten o'clock Hector reluctantly said good-night and went to bed. At five the next morning he was again with John Silver. By six o'clock in the afternoon the book was finished and Hector was at the station to meet his father. As they walked home Robert felt a crumpled paper thrust into his hand. It was THE FIREBRAND OF THE PACIFIC. Robert has never been able to determine if this was not after all THE moment of his life.

At the age of ten Hector was placed at a school of some repute in the South West of London, and three months later at the Annual Sports won the Junior Hundred Yards and Junior Quarter of a Mile scratch. Robert was pleased when he heard of the achievement, but he was no Greek, and the winning of the parsley wreath was not what he had in mind for his son; still it was gratifying to see the boy outshine his fellows.

Hector showed an ever-increasing love of outdoor sports. Cricket, football, running, jumping— nothing came amiss to him. His father watched in vain for some glimmerings of the genius that his imagination told him would develop sooner or later. His hope had been that, by means of scholarships, his son might reach Oxford or

Cambridge, for he had all the middle-class exaggerated opinion of the advantages of a University education. He saw him a senior wrangler, he saw his photograph in the papers, heard himself interviewed as to his son's early life and pursuits. From these dreams he would awaken to renewed exertions; but always with the same lack of success.

Unfortunately perhaps for both, Robert Tidmarsh saw little in his son's successes. Athletics were with him incidents in a career, incapable of being glorified into achievements. To him a judge was not a judge because he had won his blue, but rather in spite of it. He could not very well expostulate. No man, as Robert clearly saw, has a right to rebuke a son for failing to realise his father's ambitions for him. For one thing, he had no very clear idea himself what those ambitions were. All he was conscious of was a feeling that in some way or other Hector Tidmarsh was to carry on the torch that he, Robert Tidmarsh, had lighted. He was to achieve fame in some channel of life; but it must be a material fame, one that would make him a celebrity. It never occurred to Tidmarsh PÈRE that a man capable of making a century at cricket, or being the best centre-forward in the district, could be worthy of a place among a nation's contemporary worthies.

At sixteen Hector left school, regretted by masters and scholars alike, for his was a nature that commanded liking. By the influence of Mr. Ratchett, who had always been particularly partial to his chief clerk and, as an old Oxford cricket blue, was much interested in his clerk's son, Hector was articled to a solicitor. In a flash Robert Tidmarsh saw the possibility of his cherished dream being realised. He recalled instances of young men who had achieved fame in the field and subsequently become successful in the more serious walks of life. He watched the boy closely, talked to him of law, encouraged him to study, pointed out the greatness of this golden opportunity. But in vain, the boy's heart was in sport, not in law.

Sometimes in introspective moments the father examined himself as to how he had filled the role of Philip. Had he failed? Was he the cause? Could he have prevented what now appeared highly probable, the fluttering to earth of his house of cards? He had never been harsh, had he erred by being over lenient?

As he watched Hector, it slowly dawned upon him that for the first time in his life he was about to experience failure. His son was doomed to be lost in the flood of the commonplace, would be respectable, comfortably off, live at Streatham or Balham; but could never become famous. When this conviction became fixed in Robert Tidmarsh's mind, he grew gloomy and depressed. The dice had gone against him. It was fate. It is only a long line of ancestors that enables a man to play a losing game. The Tidmarsh blood lacked that tenacity and fire that comes with tradition. It remained only to wait and hope and speculate from what quarter the blow would fall.

At nineteen Hector received an invitation to play for the Surrey Colts. He "came off," making a dashing fifty. Mr. Rachett was there to shake the young giant warmly by the hand as he returned to the pavilion, but not his chief clerk. In the heart of the disappointed father there was a dull resentment against sport in general. He saw in it a siren who had bewitched his son, and diverted him from the path he should have trod. His secret was hard to keep. He needed sympathy, someone to tell him that he had done a great deal if not so much as he had anticipated.

One October morning the moment of final dis-illusionment arrived. When he came down to breakfast Hector was waiting in the dining-room with a copy of THE SPORTSMAN, which he handed to his father, at the same time pointing to a long description of a football match between two well-known league clubs; it was headed "A Man of Genius," and ran:

"The outstanding feature of the game was the marvellous display of the young amateur, Mr. Hector Tidmarsh, who was given a trial at centre forward in the home team. His pace, his subtlety, his bustling methods stamped him as a great centre-forward. The way he kept his wings together was a revelation. Time after time the quintette raced away as if opposition did not exist. The young amateur seemed to have hypnotised his professional CONFRÈRES. His shooting was equal to his feinting, and his forward-passing such as has not been seen for many a day. In short he is the greatest find of the season, or of many seasons for that matter. The directors of the − − Club are to be congratulated in having discovered a man of genius."

Robert Tidmarsh put down the paper and looked at his son; but happily bereft at the Comic Spirit, he merely articulated some commonplace words of congratulation. That morning two disappointed men commenced their breakfasts, the father realising that his cherished ideal had finally been shattered; the son depressed because a carefully planned surprise had been productive of only a few colourless words, and upon them both smiled a proud wife and happy mother, to whom fame for those she loved, be it in what form it may, was a great and glorious gift to be welcomed with laughter and with tears.

I lay aside the manuscript and proceeded to light a cigarette. As a rule at the end of a reading there is a babel of comment. To-night there was an unusual silence. I looked round the room. There was a far-away look in Sallie's eyes, which seemed unusually bright. Dick Little was gazing straight in front of him, Bindle was recharging his pipe with great deliberation and care. The Boy was lost in the contemplation of his finger nails.

"Silly ass!"

It was Angell Herald who had broken the silence, and snapped the thread. All eyes turned in his direction. Bindle, who was just in the act of lighting his pipe, paused and gazed curiously at Angell Herald over the flame of the match, then he turned to me and I saw that he understood.

It was Windover, however, who expressed the opinion of the Club upon Angell Herald's comment, when he muttered loud enough for all to hear:

"Oh! for the jawbone of an ass!"

CHAPTER IX
MRS. BILTOX-JONES'S EXPERIMENT

I do not think any of us really liked Angell Herald, his self-satisfied philistinism constituting a serious barrier to close personal relations. I have already commented upon certain of his characteristics that jarred upon us all; but it seemed no one's business to indicate, delicately or otherwise, that he was not so welcome as we might have wished.

Dick Little had introduced him on the strength of a story he had heard him tell at some masonic dinner, I think it was, and he had decided that Angell Herald would be an acquisition to the Night Club. Sallie thought otherwise, and had summed him up as "a worm in a top hat": he always wore a top hat. It was the only occasion on which I had known Sallie break out into epigram. Both she and Bindle disliked Angell Herald almost to the point of intolerance. As a matter of fact he is not a bad fellow, if his foibles are not too much emphasized.

His principal asset, however, is that he has a fund of interesting experiences which, strangely enough, he rates far lower than the stories he at first would insist on telling.

He assured us that Mrs. Biltox-Jones was no imaginary person and we, knowing his limitations, believed him, and that her social experiment was at the time the talk of Fleet Street.

I

"Damn the war!" exclaimed Angell Herald, leaning back in his chair and looking at his clerk, who had just entered.

"Yes sir," said Pearl, in a non-committal manner. There are moments when Pearl rises almost to inspiration. His sympathetic utterance was balm to his employer's anguished soul.

Pearl accepts his chief's moods or reflects them, whichever seems the more expedient at the moment. Incidentally Pearl has a heart that filled the War Office with foreboding; so Pearl will never become a V.C.

When Angell Herald uttered his impulsive remark, with which Pearl had so tactfully concurred, he had just finished reading a letter from Messrs. Simoon, Golbrith and Cathpell, Ltd. It consisted of three lines; but those three lines had brushed away a hundred a year from his income. This is what they wrote:—

"To Angell Herald, Esq.,
        Publicity Agent,

382, Fleet Street, E.C.

DEAR SIR,

We regret to inform you that on account of the war we shall not be able to renew our advertising contract for the current year.

We are,

Yours faithfully,

(Signed) SIMOON, GOLBRITH & CATHPELL, LTD.

There was not a word of sympathy with the unfortunate publicity agent for his loss, no touch of humanity or pity, merely a bare announcement, and Angell Herald felt he was justified in saying, as he did say with a great deal of emphasis, "Damn the war!"

He fell to brooding over this letter. Publicity agents had been very badly hit by the war, and he foresaw the time when— well, anything might happen. He was awakened from his gloom by Pearl.

"I've got a friend, sir— — "

"I know you have, Pearl," was the response. "You have too many friends. That's the infernal part of it. You are always marrying or burying them."

"I have a friend," continued Pearl, imperturbably, "who says that new conditions demand new methods."

Angell Herald sat up straight, and looked at Pearl. Knowing him as his employer did, this was a most extraordinary utterance. There was in it just a spark of originality.

"Pearl," said Angell Herald, "you've been drinking."

"No, sir," he replied, seriously, "I never take any alcoholic stimulant until after dinner."

"Then you have a funeral in mind," was the reply. "Something has intoxicated you."

Pearl seemed to deliberate for a moment and then replied,

"Well, sir, I was going to tell you that my aunt's second husband has had a stroke, and he is not expected to live. We are planning the funeral for Thursday week."

Angell Herald felt that the loss of the Simoon contract had, as far as business was concerned, done him for the day, so he went out, bought a rose, and got his hat ironed. He then turned into "The Turkey Trot" and played a game of dominoes with his friend Harry Trumpet, who represents the old school of publicity men: he calls himself an advertising agent. He is a dull and stereotyped fellow, and, when Angell Herald feels at all depressed, it always puts him in countenance with himself to come in contact with Harry Trumpet.

"Harry is an ass," Angell Herald had once said; "but the amusing thing is that he doesn't know it. I once met his wife and his wife's sister, and they don't seem to know it either."

Having evaded Trumpet's very obvious readiness to be invited to lunch, Angell Herald went to his favourite place and did himself as well as he could. He was just drinking the last drop of claret, when Pearl's remark came back to him. He remembered the old French saying "autre temps, autre moeurs." It was the only piece of French that he could recollect, save the words "cocotte" and "très femme."

His mind wandered back to that "interview" with Mr. Llewellyn John, who had given him such infinite instruction in the art of advertising.

It was, however, the agony column of THE AGE that gave him his inspiration. There he saw an advertisement, which read:—
"A lady of considerable wealth desires introduction into Society. A stranger to London. Apply in the first instance in strict confidence to X.Q. Box 38432. The office of THE AGE, Paper Buildings Quadrangle, E.C."
"A munition fortune," Angell Herald muttered to himself. "She has made her money, the old dear, and now she wants to get into high society, and wash away the taste of Guinness in the flavour of Moet and Chandon. In other words, she wants publicity."

The word "publicity" suggested himself. Here was a woman desirous of publicity, here was Angell Herald wanting nothing better than to get for people publicity.

He returned to his office.

"Pearl," he said, "you can have that half holiday on Thursday week. I think you have given me an idea."

"Thank you, sir," was his reply, and Pearl proceeded to ask for a rise, which was instantly refused, his chief telling him that time was money.

Angell Herald wrote a guarded letter to the lady desiring entry into high society, telling her that he thought he might possibly be of some assistance if she would kindly allow him the privilege of calling upon her. He received an equally guarded reply, making an appointment at the office of a certain firm of solicitors in Lincoln's Inn.

II

Three days later Angell Herald was sitting in a room in the offices of Messrs. Robbe & Dammitt, the well-known society solicitors, awaiting the arrival of his fair client— as he hoped. He was meditating upon the old-fashioned methods of solicitors as he gazed round the room with its dusty volumes of law books, its hard, uncompromising chairs, and its long, stamped-leather covered office table, when the door opened, and there sailed in— sailed is really the only expression that conveys the motion— a heavily veiled female figure. As he rose and bowed he recalled Dick Grassetts' description of his mother-in-law, "All front and no figure served up in black silk."

"Mr. Herald?" she interrogated in a husky voice, flopping down into a chair with a gasp.

Angell Herald bowed.

For fully a minute she sat panting. Evidently the short flight of stairs had been too much for her.

"You saw my advertisement?" she queried.

Again Angell Herald bowed.

"Well, what about it?" she enquired. Her attitude was one of extreme arrogance, which was oddly out of keeping with the inflection of her voice and the directness of her speech. Obviously she was determined to assume the attitude of the theatrical duchess. It was necessary to put her in her place.

"I saw your advertisement," Angell Herald remarked, "and remembering what Mr. Llewellyn John said to me the other day— — "

"Mr. Llewellyn John," she gasped. "You know him?"

"Oh, yes," Angell Herald replied, airily. "As I was saying, he remarked to me the other day, 'Without advertisement a man is doomed.' That gave me the idea of writing to you."

"Yes, go on," she said eagerly, as she raised her veil.

"Well, madam," Angell Herald continued, "you require certain social opportunities," she nodded her head vigorously and gasped like a fat pug that sees tempting dainties it is too full to eat, "and I think I may be able to be of some assistance."

Angell Herald did not like the woman. Her complexion was blue, her face puffy, and she had innumerable chins, which billowed down to meet the black silk of her gown. She was hung with jewellery, and her clothes were most unsuitable to her years. In her hat was mauve and emerald green. She was literally laden with sables, which must have considerably increased her difficulty in breathing, and her feet were pinched into the most ridiculously small patent boots with enormous tassels that bobbed about every time she moved. Although a man of the world, Angell Herald was appalled at the shortness of her skirts.

She blinked at him through her lorgnettes.

"Well!" she said.

"May I enquire first of all," he enquired, "what methods you have hitherto adopted? I may tell you that everything discussed between us is in strict confidence."

This seemed to reassure her. After a slight hesitation she began to tell her story. It appeared that her husband had made an enormous fortune in the early days of the war by contracting for porous huts and brown-paper boots for the Army. They had lived in Manchester, but now they had come to London and taken what was literally a mansion in Park Lane. She had set herself to work to get into Society, and apparently had been very badly snubbed.

She had subscribed liberally to the Red Cross and similar charities, and attended every charitable entertainment that had been given since her advent. She had engaged, regardless of cost, a number of the most famous artists in the country for a drawing-room concert in aid of a certain hospital, and had sent out invitations lavishly to the whole of Mayfair. The result was that the artists had turned up; but not the audience.

She had to pay the fees and eat the leek. Then she had offered to drive convalescent soldiers round the Park.

"And they sent me common soldiers," she remarked, "although I particularly asked for officers, generals if possible." There was a note of querulous complaint in her voice.

It was with something akin to horror that Angell Herald heard her say she had written to THE AGE, asking what their terms would be to publish a photograph of her daughter, together with a few personal particulars.

"THE AGE, madam?" he almost shrieked. "THE AGE? They never publish illustrations."

"No," she replied. "But they publish advertisements and theatrical notices. My daughter (she pronounced it 'darter') is as good as a music-hall actress, and a good sight better," she added.

She had left cards on everyone in Park Lane, (she called it "The Lane"), and upon a number of people in other fashionable quarters, but had not received a single call in return.

"Your only chance, madam," Angell Herald ventured, "is to get into the public eye. These are the days of advertisement. You must get the public to know you as they know our generals and our politicians."

"I know all about that," she replied, with a certain asperity. "But how's it going to be done?"

"Well!" Angell Herald replied, "I will think it over and let you know. Perhaps you will tell me to whom I can write."

For a moment she hesitated, and then saying, "Of course the whole thing's strictly in confidence?" Angell Herald bowed— she handed him her card. On it he read "Mrs. Biltox-Jones, 376, Park Lane, W.," and in the corner "Third Thursdays." Angell Herald smiled inwardly as he thought of the loneliness of this lady on her "Third Thursdays."

For a minute or two he gazed reflectively at Mrs. Biltox-Jones's card. Through his mind was running the "interview" with Mr. Llewellyn John. He remembered the suggestion of the accident in stepping into his car, how the Prime Minister had suggested that he should be assaulted for purposes of publicity, and finally he recalled the suggestion of the abduction of his daughter. Without pausing to think, he turned to Mrs. Biltox-Jones.

"You have a daughter, Mrs. Biltox-Jones?" he said, taking great care to give her her hyphenated name.

She started.

"A daughter!" she said. "Of course I've got a daughter." Her tone was that of someone accused of lacking some necessary member.

"Exactly," he said. "That may solve the difficulty. In these days," he continued, "publicity is a very difficult matter." Angell Herald put his fingers together in judicial fashion and proceeded, "There are two things that the journalist recognises. One is 'copy,' Mrs. Biltox-Jones, and the other is 'news.' Now news takes precedence over 'copy,' just as birth does over money, at least, it should do."

"I don't see what that's got to do with the matter at all," snapped Mrs. Biltox-Jones. Angell Herald could see that she had not formed a very favourable opinion of him, or of his capabilities. "I don't understand what you mean by 'copy' and 'news.'"

"Well," he continued, "I once heard a journalist define the two." Ha was quite indifferent as to what Mrs. Biltox-Jones might think of him. "A friend once asked him the same question, and his reply was, 'Now, if a dog bit a man, that would be 'copy'; but, Mrs. Biltox-Jones, if a man bit a dog, that would be 'news.'"

Mrs. Biltox-Jones was clearly annoyed. She made a movement to rise; but to rise, with Mrs. Biltox-Jones, was a matter of several movements, persistent and sustained.

"One moment, madam," Angell Herald continued. "In your own case, now, in order to obtain the publicity you desire, you must endeavour to give the Press something that it will regard as 'news' in distinction from 'copy.' Now, as far as I can see, there are two ways in which you can achieve your object."

Mrs. Biltox-Jones began to look interested once more.

"First you might arrange to be seriously assaulted."

"Me?" she gasped. "Me, assaulted? What on earth do you mean, Mr. Herald?"

"Well," he continued, "You might arrange for somebody to meet you in a lonely place, and knock you down."

"Knock ME down?" The italics fail to do justice to Mrs. Biltox-Jones's look and tone. "Are you mad?" she demanded.

"No," was the response. "I am endeavouring to help you. If you will listen calmly, you will see what I'm driving at. The fact of a lady of your position and wealth being publicly assaulted would appeal to the journalistic mind, and would undoubtedly result in a great deal of Press notice."

"But it would be so painful," she replied.

"Of course, there is always that. It might even be fatal. There is, of course, an alternative measure, which I think, in your case, might be even better: that is, the abduction of your daughter."

"The what?" she shrieked.

"The abduction of Miss Biltox-Jones. Imagine the sensation! Think of the 'copy'! Millionaire's daughter abducted— I assume Mr. Biltox-Jones is a millionaire. I believe all Army contractors who are business men have become millionaires. Yes," Angell Herald added, "I think Miss Biltox-Jones might be abducted."

"That shows you don't know Gertie," said Mrs. Biltox-Jones, smiling grimly. At least, she made certain facial movements which were intended to indicate a smile.

Mrs. Biltox-Jones seemed to be thinking deeply. After fully a minute's silence she demanded, rather truculently,

"Will you abduct her?"

Angell Herald drew himself up with dignity.

"I am a publicity agent, Mrs. Biltox-Jones, not a professional abductor of millionaires' daughters. Furthermore I have a reputation to maintain."

"All right, don't get 'uffy," was her response.

Angell Herald shuddered.

Again there was silence between them.

"Gertie's always complainin' how dull she is," Mrs. Biltox-Jones muttered to herself; "she might like it for a change. P'raps Martin might arrange it. Martin's my butler, he does everythink for me. He's been with the Duke of Porchester, and Prince Carmichael of Dam-Splititz."

"Well," Angell Herald proceeded. "Let us see Miss Biltox-Jones abducted. Imagine the Press the next morning. You would apply to the police, you would intimate the terrible news to every newspaper, and there would be scare headings. I merely offer this as a suggestion. As a matter of fact, it is a little out of my usual line of business. New conditions, however, Mrs. Biltox-Jones, demand new methods." Angell Herald blessed Pearl for that exquisite phrase, and registered a vow not to refuse his next application for a holiday in which to bury, marry or bail-out a friend. He could almost see himself giving him a rise.

"But how could I do it?" she enquired.

"That," Angell Herald replied, "I must leave to you, Mrs. Biltox-Jones. I should gather that you are not lacking in resource or originality. I should try Martin. English butlers are wonderfully resourceful. Get your daughter abducted and the result will be that your name will be sounded throughout the British Empire. I may add, by the way, that I should see she was abducted for at least a fortnight. That would give time for a thorough Press campaign. You would find that all the Colonial papers would copy the story, and if Miss Biltox-Jones happened to be handsome, as I should imagine she would be"— Angell Herald looked very pointedly at Mrs. Biltox-Jones, and she preened herself like a second-hand peacock— "then the sensation created would be the greater.

"I am afraid, madam, that I can do nothing more than make this suggestion; but you may be assured that if you act upon it, you will not lack the publicity that I gather all ladies of your position seek."

For a few moments she was silent, then said, "And what's all this cost, Mr. Herald?"

"Oh," he replied, "it's a very trifling matter. Let us say fifty guineas, shall we, especially as I am not able to be of any practical assistance to you."

"I'll send you a cheque." Her jaw snapped with a determined air that convinced Angell Herald that in the very near future Miss Biltox-Jones would be abducted.

III

A little over a week later, Angell Herald had left the office to get his usual simple lunch of everything the food restrictions permitted, and as much in the way of extras as he could squeeze in, when his eye was arrested by a placard of THE EVENING MAIL. He had already received a cheque for fifty guineas from Mrs. Biltox-Jones, and had dismissed the circumstance from his memory. This placard, however, brought back the whole story vividly to his recollection. It read

ATTEMPTED ABDUCTION

AN AMAZON FEAT

Something seemed to link up that newspaper placard with the fifty guinea cheque, and he purchased THE EVENING MAIL.

On the front page of the paper, most of which seemed to be covered with clever headlines, he read the following with something akin to amazement:

ATTEMPTED ABDUCTION OP A MILLIONAIRE'S DAUGHTER

A MODERN AMAZON

SOCIETY YOUNG LADY OUTWITS TWO DESPERATE RUFFIANS

THE ABDUCTORS CAPTURED

AN AMAZING FEAT

"Last evening, about 9.15, Miss Biltox-Jones, the daughter of Mr. and Mrs. Jeremiah Biltox-Jones, of 376 Park Lane, W., was motoring back from Epsom, where she had been lunching with friends, when her car was stopped by someone waving a red light on the middle of the road. The chauffeur, seeing the danger-signal, immediately pulled up, and a moment afterwards, to his astonishment, found a pistol presented to his head, and he was told that if he moved a muscle he would be shot.

"It was afterwards discovered that two masked men were responsible for this outrage. The second man approached the car, and invited Miss Biltox-Jones to alight, which she accordingly did. He then informed her that she was his prisoner, and would be taken away to await the payment of a ransom. But they had reckoned without their host, or shall we say hostess. It appears that Miss Biltox-Jones is an adept at physical culture, ju jitsu and such like things. With a swift movement she had her attacker on his back upon the road; hitting him smartly on the temple with the butt-end of his own pistol, she rendered him unconscious, and before the other ruffian was aware of what had happened, she had floored him likewise.

"With the aid of the chauffeur, the two men were bound, placed in the car, and taken to the nearest police-station. They are to appear this morning before the magistrate, the outrage having taken place on the outskirts of London, when further particulars of this strange affair will probably be divulged.

"In the meantime we congratulate Miss Biltox-Jones on what must be regarded as a remarkable achievement."

There followed an interview with the chauffeur; another interview with Miss Biltox-Jones, together with her portrait. She proved to be a not uncomely girl of muscular proportions and determined expression.

For a moment Angell Herald was dazed at the turn events had taken. He inwardly cursed Pearl and his ridiculous advice. He saw himself involved in a most unsavoury business. He even wondered why he had not been sent for to attend the police-court proceedings. What was he to do? There was nothing for it but to wait for subsequent editions of the paper.

Engagements prevented him from returning to the office until nearly six. As he entered he saw that Pearl was in a state of suppressed excitement. He too had read the wretched story.

"Mrs. Biltox-Jones to see you, sir."

"What?" Angell Herald almost shouted.

"She's been here three-quarters of an hour, sir. She insisted on waiting."

Never had Angell Herald felt such a coward. Why had he not foreseen that she would descend upon him. Could he turn and fly? No: a man must appear a hero before his own clerk. He would lose for ever Pearl's respect if he were to flee at that moment.

Assuming an air of nonchalance, he said he would see Mrs. Biltox-Jones immediately, and, with shaking hand, opened the door of his room, prepared for a blast of reproach such as it had never been his fate to experience.

To his utter bewilderment, Mrs. Biltox-Jones was sitting smiling, and, more wonderful still, holding in her hand a cheque, which she extended to him, as she made certain bouncing movements, which he rightly interpreted as preliminaries to her assuming an upright position.

Utterly bewildered, he took the cheque, What could be the meaning of this new development? Instinctively he looked at the cheque; it was for a hundred guineas. Clearly Mrs. Biltox-Jones was mad.

"Mr. Herald," she began, in her wheezy voice, having got to her feet, "you've done me a real service, you've got me what I wanted. You're a wonderful man."

"But— but— " he stammered.

"No, no," she continued. "No modesty. The idea was entirely yours. Of course I didn't anticipate Gertie upsetting things like that; but then you never know what Gertie will do, and the poor child so enjoyed it."

Angell Herald pictured the Gertie whose photograph he had seen, "enjoying it." Then his thoughts turned to the nefarious abductors.

"But the men," he asked, "Who were they?"

"Oh! Martin arranged that. One was his brother, and the other was John's second cousin. John is my first footman. But, of course, a great general has to be prepared for everything, as you said the other day." (Angell Herald had no recollection of saying anything of the sort.) "So when I heard these two men had been caught by Gertie, I decided to turn the whole thing into a joke. Gertie was delighted, and said that she hadn't enjoyed anything so for a long time. The magistrate, of course, was most rude about it."

"But the butler's brother and the— "

"They've been released. The magistrate pitched into them; but still, it's all right, although Martin's brother has a big bump on his head, which will cost a good deal, and John's cousin can be squared. The teeth he lost were not really his own, although he said they were until I threatened to ring up my dentist and have his mouth examined."

"Yes," she continued, after a pause, "it was really a brilliant idea of yours, Mr. Herald, and I thank you for it. I shall recommend you to my friends. My husband has great influence in the city, and he shall know what a remarkable man you are."

"And," began Angell Herald, "have the er— er— — "

"Oh! I've had heaps of callers. Sir Jacob and Lady Wanderlust, Mrs. Hermann Schmidt, Mr. Gottinhimmel, Mr. Lüftstoessel, Miss Strafestein, and a lot of the best people in The Lane. And they're so patriotic. They do SO hate the Kaiser, and they simply LOVE England. We have become great friends."

Angell Herald congratulated her. "And now I must be going," she said, "I've got to arrange about compensating those two poor men. If you knew Gertie as I know her, you'd know they didn't come off without severe er— er— contoosions, was what the doctor called 'em."

Mrs. Biltox-Jones sailed out of the office wheezing and smiling. Angell Herald saw Pearl looking at him in a bewildered fashion, and he almost fainted when handed the cheque and told to pay it into the bank.

The late evening papers were full of this extraordinary "joke." By a lucky chance, there was no news from anywhere. The German Emperor had not been patronizing the Almighty, and no one had shown on any of the fronts the least inclination to push. The result was that the photographs of the Biltox-Joneses, of their butler, the butler's brother, of John, and John's second cousin, filled every newspaper. The scene of the "outrage" was pictured, with a cross marking the spot on the road where Martin's brother's head had been tapped.

In Angell Herald's heart there was a great gladness and a deep gratitude to Mr. Llewellyn John! He had the greatest difficulty to restrain himself from giving Pearl a rise.— Instead he gave him the cigar he had received from Trumpet a few days previously. There are no half tones about either Trumpet or his cigars.

At the conclusion of the story Angell Herald, sat back with the air of a man prepared to receive the congratulations that he knows are his due. He was obviously disappointed when the only remark made was Sallie's.

"Poor old thing."

"I should like to meet that clerk of 'is," "whispered" Bindle to Windover. "'E ought to be able to tell us some things, wot?"

"Ha, yes," muttered Windover abstractedly, "but it's casting Pearls before swine though."

CHAPTER X
THE NIGHT CLUB VISITS BINDLE

One Sunday evening on arriving at Dick Little's flat I was greeted with the announcement "J.B.'s ill." I looked round at the gloomy faces. It was then that I appreciated how the Night Club revolved round Bindle's personality.

From a note Dick Little had received it appeared that Bindle had hurt his ankle and been forced to lie up for a week. His letter was characteristic. It ran:—

"DEAR SIR,

I been kicking what I didn't ought to have kicked, and I got to lay up for a week. Cheero! I shall think of the Night Club.

Yours respectfully,

JOE BINDLE."

We wondered what it was that Bindle had kicked that he ought not to have kicked. There was, we felt sure, a story behind the letter.

We looked at each other rather helplessly.

"Shall we begin?" asked Angell Herald. One of his stories was down for that evening.

"We must wait for Miss Carruthers," said Jim Owen, a cousin of mine and rather an ass about women.

At that moment Sallie and Jack Carruthers turned up and were told the direful news.

"Oh! poor J.B.," cried Sallie, who had quite drifted into our way of speech.

"What shall we do?" asked Jack Carruthers.

We all looked at each other as if expectant of a solution anywhere but in our own brains.

"I have it!" cried Sallie suddenly clapping her hands, her eyes flashing with excitement.

"Out with it, Sallie," said Jack, putting his arm round her shoulders. Many of us envied him that habit of his.

"We'll all go and see J.B.," cried Sallie.

Dick Little nearly got notice to quit through that idea of Sallie's. The yell that went up to the ceiling above was as nothing to the things that fell from the ceiling below. Tom Little was in a mad mood, and he insisted that we should all form a ring round Sallie, and hand in hand we flung ourselves round her; "flung" was the only word that describes our motions. There were sixteen of us, and Dick Little's rooms are not over large. It was a mad rout.

We were interrupted in our acclamation of Sallie's inspiration by a tremendous hammering at the door of the flat. Dick Little opened it and let in a flood of the most exotic language to which we had ever listened. It was talk that would have made a drill-sergeant envious. It had about it the tang of the barrack-square. It silenced us and stilled our movements as nothing else would have done. It poured in through the door like a flood. It gave an intensely personal view of ourselves, our forebears and our posterity, if any. It described our education, our up-bringing and the inadequacy of the penal code of England. We stood in hushed admiration, especially the men from Tim's.

Sallie listened for about half a minute, quite unperturbed. It is a strange thing; but "language" has no effect on Sallie. I have seen her listening quite gravely to the inspired utterances of a Thames lighterman. This evening, at the end of half a minute, she walked to the door, we crowding behind her to see the fun, for we had all recognised the voice of General Burdett-Coombe, who lived immediately beneath Dick Little. Suddenly the General's eloquence stopped. He had seen Sallie.

"Won't you come in," she said looking at him gravely, with eyes a little larger and a little grayer than usual.

"I— I— " stammered the General, then seeing us all gazing at him he burst out.

"God bless my soul, what on earth have I done? I had no idea there was a lady here. I— I— "

"Please come in," said Sallie, "I want you to tell these men how horribly badly behaved they are. You were doing it quite nicely; but I am afraid they didn't hear it all."

The General looked from Sallie to the men, who had now streamed out and were filling Dick Little's small hall. Then seeing Sallie smile he suddenly burst out laughing, showing a set of dazzlingly white teeth beneath his grizzled grey moustache.

"Routed, by heaven! routed and by a woman. My dear young lady," he said, turning to Sallie, "I owe you a thousand apologies. I— I'm afraid I rather let myself go. These young hooligans have knocked down my electrolier. I thought the whole blessed place was coming on my head," and he laughed again out of sheer boyish enjoyment.

From that day Sallie and General Burdett-Coombe became great friends, and that was how it happened that the General came to join the Night Club.

As he went down to his flat he once more apologised; but Sallie said that he was quite justified in what he had said and done.

"Well, well," he cried after a swift glance to see if she were pulling his leg, "Boys will be boys I suppose; but I wish they would leave my electrolier alone. Good-night all," and the chorus of "good-nights" was almost as great in volume as the shouts that had greeted Sallie's inspiration.

"Now then you fellows, taxis," cried Tom Little.

Three men dashed downstairs to commandeer all the taxis in the neighbourhood. Tom Little and Bill Simmonds disappeared; but the rest of us managed the crowd into the four taxis that were available. As we sped along to Fenton Street, Fulham, where Bindle lives, each empty taxi that approached was hailed and some of the party got out and entered. Eventually when we arrived at Fenton Street the procession numbered eight vehicles.

The sensation we caused will go down to posterity as the greatest day in the annals of the district. Neighbours flocked to their doors. Gramophones, which were tinnily striving to reproduce masterpieces they had mis-heard, were allowed to run down, and soon what portion of the street that was not occupied by taxis was filled with open-mouthed residents.

The general impression was that it was a police raid, although how they reconciled Sallie with the police was difficult to understand.

Just as we were knocking at Bindle's door, Tom Little and Bill Simmonds arrived in a ninth vehicle, out of which they hauled two large suit-cases.

The door of Bindle's house was opened by Ginger, who looked his astonishment at seeing Sallie with some sixteen men behind her.

"Is Mr. Bindle in?" enquired Sallie.

Without attempting to reply Ginger called over his shoulder, "Someone to see yer, Joe."

"Ask 'im in," came the cheery voice of Bindle from within.

"It ain't 'im, it's a lady."

"Come along in, Martha, I know 'oo it is."

Sallie passed by the open-mouthed Ginger, and we trooped in behind her. Bindle was lying on a horse-hair couch with one ankle heavily bandaged. His back was towards the door; but he called out over his shoulders, "Come in, Martha, come in. 'Ow's yer breath and 'ow's 'Earty?"

"It's me," said Sallie, regardless as to grammar.

Bindle looked round as if someone had shot him from behind, saw Sallie and the rest of us behind her.

"Gawd Almighty," he exclaimed in utter astonishment. "I'm blowed if it ain't the Night Club. Cheero! the lot," and "the lot" cheero-d Bindle.

Tom Little and Bill Simmonds then came forward with their suit-cases. From these they produced what appeared to be an endless stream of refreshments: bottles of beer, two bottles of whisky, a dozen syphons of soda and a miscellaneous assortment of sandwiches such as are to be found on public-house counters. For once in his life Bindle's speech failed him, as he watched the kitchen table being turned into a sort of public-house bar. Then slowly a happy grin spread over his face and looking up at Sallie, who had come and stood beside him, said,

"This'll do me more good than all the doctor's stuff, miss."

I looked at Bindle closely, the voice was so unlike his. Before leaving Dick Little's flat, Sallie had collected all the flowers that she could find, which she carried in a big bouquet. Dick Little is fond of flowers.

"Is them flowers for the coffin, miss," enquired Bindle, with a strange twist of a smile.

"They're for Mrs. Bindle," said Sallie with inspiration.

"Well, I'm— Hi, stop 'im, don't let 'im go." Bindle's eyes had caught sight of Ginger, who was slipping out of the door.

Jack Carruthers made a grab and caught the delinquent by the sleeve. Ginger seemed inclined to show fight; but three or four of Tim's men soon persuaded his that God is always on the side of the big battalions, and Ginger was led back into the room.

"Ginger," said Bindle, reprovingly, "I'm surprised at you. When Miss Sallie comes to see us, you go sneaking off as if you'd picked 'er pocket, or owed 'er money. Wot jer mean by it?"

"I don't 'old wiv— — " began Ginger.

"Never mind what you 'old with, Ging, you've got to stand by and see your old pal ain't choked with all these good things."

A fugitive shaft of light came into Ginger's eyes as he saw the array of bottles on the kitchen table. Tom Little and Bill Simmonds were busy commandeering all the glasses, cups, mugs, etc., they could find on the dresser, and unscrewing the tops of the beer bottles.

"Ow jer come?" enquired Bindle while these preparations were in progress.

"Taxis," I replied mechanically, "There are nine of them waiting outside."

"Nine?" exclaimed Bindle, his eyes open to their full extent. "Nine taxis in Fenton Street? 'Old be 'Orace!" and he laughed till the tears poured down his cheeks. Bindle was in a mood to laugh at anything.

"An' wot's all the neighbours doin', sir."

"Oh! they're busy counting them," said Carruthers, "they think it's a police raid." This was one of the few occasions on which I have seen Bindle laugh, as a rule he grins. Presently, wiping his eyes with the corner of a newspaper he had been reading, he cried "'Ere, a glass of milk for the invalid."

Tom Little dashed for the largest jug and filled it up with such haste that the froth foamed down the sides. Bindle clutched the jug with both hands.

"Excuse my getting up, miss, but 'eres to the Night Club."

We all joined in the toast.

"I wonder wot Mrs. B.'ll think of it all when she comes back," remarked Bindle. "Nine taxis an' a police raid. They're sure to tell 'er."

The seating accommodation in Bindle's kitchen was limited. A chair was found for Sallie, and several more were brought out of the adjoining parlour; but most of us sat on the floor. Windover occupied one end of the fender and Angell Herald the other. The comparison between the two was interesting. Windover sat as if all his life had been spent on the end of a fender, Angell Herald, on the other hand, as if he meant everybody to understand that never before had he found himself so situated. Windover was enjoying himself, Angell Herald was acutely uncomfortable. He knew it must be all right by the fact of Windover being there; but his whole appearance seemed to convey the fact that he was unaccustomed to sitting on a fender with a china mug of whisky and soda in one hand, and a ham sandwich of public-house proportions in the other.

Windover seemed to find a quiet enjoyment in the situation.

"How did you hurt your foot, Mr. Bindle?" enquired Sallie.

"Oh! I jest kicked up against somethink wot I didn't ought to 'ave kicked, miss," was Bindle's response.

To further questioning he was evasive. It was clear that he did not wish to tell us what had happened. It was equally clear that Sallie was determined to know.

"Why don't you tell 'em, Joe, what you did?" It was Ginger who broke in. A different Ginger from him who had endeavoured to slip out of the room, a Ginger mellowed by three bottles of beer. Finding the whole attention of the room centred upon Bindle, Ginger buried his head in a large milk jug from which he was drinking.

"Look 'ere, Ging, you keep that muzzle on. You ain't no talker."

Sallie-turned to Ginger, who had already fallen a victim to her eyes. "Please Mr.— Mr.— "

And then it was I remembered that no one had ever heard Ginger's name.

"We call 'im Ginger, miss; but you mustn't let 'im talk. 'E's some'ow out of the way of it."

"Please Mr. Ginger, tell us what happened?"

Bindle made a motion as if to stop Ginger, who replaced the jug on the table and wiped his lips with the back of his disengaged hand.

"It was down at the yard, miss. Ruddy Bill tied a tin on to Polly's kitten's tail."

"But— but— " said Sallie, "I don't understand." She looked from Ginger to Bindle.

"You are an ole 'uggins," said Bindle to Ginger. "Yer couldn't keep that face of yours shut, could yer? It's like this, miss. There's a little kid down at the yard wot's got a kitten, all fluffy fur, and Ruddy Bill tied a tin on to the poor thing's tail, an' it went almost mad with fright, so— so my foot sort o' came up against Ruddy Bill. 'E wouldn't fight, you see."

"Ruddy Bill's in the 'firmary," rumbled Ginger.

"Yes, an' I'm on the couch."

Never had the Bindles' kitchen witnessed a scene such as that on which the Night Club descended upon it. Even Ginger's gloom was mitigated under the influence of the talk and good fellowship, assisted by unlimited beer. The kitchen floor was covered with men and mugs, glasses and bottles of whisky and syphons of soda. The atmosphere was grey with tobacco smoke, and the air full of the sound of half a dozen separate conversations.

Bindle had never looked happier. Every now and then he cast his eyes round in the direction of the door. His dramatic instinct told him that the culmination of the evening's festivities would synchronise with Mrs. Bindle's advent.

"You'll stay an' see Mrs. B., miss, won't yer," said Bindle to Sallie. "She's been a bit poorly of late. I think 'er soul is 'urtin' 'er more'n usual."

"Mr. Bindle," said Sallie severely, "you must not tease her. You must smooth things, not make them rougher."

"I don't understand women, miss," he replied, then after a pause he continued, "There's one thing yer can always be sure about, an' that is no matter wot yer think a woman's goin' to do, she's bound to give yer a bit of a surprise."

"As how?" enquired the Boy.

"Well, it won't do yer no 'arm to learn, you wi' that smile o' yours." The Boy grew scarlet. "You're in for trouble, Mr. 'Indenburg, sure as sure."

"What is in your mind," enquired Carruthers. We all like to hear Bindle on women.

"I was thinkin' o' that air-raid, last Saturday," he replied. "Now Mrs. Bindle, although she knows that death will be 'a release from the fetters of the flesh,' as she puts it, yet when she 'eard the guns she bolted into the coal-cellar as if 'er soul was as shaky as mine. When I gets 'ome there she was a settin' on a chair in the kitchen a-'oldin' of 'er 'eart, 'er face all white where it wasn't black from the coal."

"And what did you do, Mr. Bindle?" enquired Sallie, leaning forward with eager interest. Sallie has a theory that in reality Bindle is very considerate and thoughtful in regard to Mrs. Bindle.

"Well, miss," said Bindle after a momentary hesitation, "I give 'er three goes o' whisky an' water."

"But I thought she was temperance," broke in Dare.

"She WAS, sir," was the reply. "When she'd lapped up the last o' the third go, which finished up the 'alf quartern, she turns on me an' she jest gives me pickles."

"But why?" enquired Sallie.

"She said I done it a-purpose, makin' 'er break the pledge, an' that Gawd didn't ought to blame 'er, 'cause she was married to an 'eathen. Funny 'er not thinkin' of it before she'd 'ad the lot, that's wot does me.

"Talkin' of air raids," he continued after a pause, "it's funny 'ow they seem to affect them as are surest of gettin' an 'arp an' trimmin's, while they leaves the 'eathen merry and bright. Now me an' Ginger was on the tail o' the van when the 'Uns' little 'ummin' birds started a-layin' eggs. People yelled to 'im to get under cover: but the 'orses was scared, an' 'e goes to 'old their 'eads an' talk to 'em in that miserable way of 'is. Them 'orses was never so glad in all their lives to 'ear ole Ginger's voice."

"And what did you do, J.B.?" enquired the Boy with interest.

Bindle turned and looked him full in the face. "I ain't in this story, Mr. Clever 'Indenburg. You can think o' me as under the van. Ginger was jest as cool as wot you was when you got that bit o' ribbon for your tunic."

The expression in the Boy's face was evidence that Bindle had scored.

"Now take 'Earty," Bindle continued, "'E's one o' them wot's got a front row ticket for 'eaven; yet when the guns begins to go off, and the bombs was droppin', 'e nips down into the potato-cellar 'to take stock', although 'e 'adn't 'ad a potato there for months. Took 'im quite a long time it did too, takin' stock o' nothink. There was poor ole Martha left to look after the shop. Rummy card 'Earty. 'E's afraid o' too much joy, thinks it might sort o' get to 'is 'ead. 'E's nuts on 'eaven an' angels; but it's business as usual as long as 'e can.

"No," Bindle continued after a pause in which to take a pull at his tankard and recharge and light his pipe, "the longer I lives the less I seems to know about people. There's Mrs. B. 'oo's always sayin' that 'the way o' the transgressor is 'ard', yet look at me! I'm always cheerio, but she's mostly like a camel wot's jest found another 'ump a-growin'.

"No one don't never seem able to understand another cove's way o' lookin' at things. I 'ad a sister once, pretty gal she was, too, got it from me I expect. I used to get quite a lot o' free beer from my mates wot wanted me to put in a good word with Annie. Seemed funny like to me that they should want to 'ang round 'er when there was other gals about.

"Yes," continued Bindle after a pause, "there's a lot o' things I don't understand. Look at them young women a-gaddin' about the West-End when it's war an' 'ell for our boys out there. Sometimes I'd like to ask 'em wot they mean."

"They're cultivating the present so that the future shall not find them without a past," murmured Windover.

"Nietzsche says that woman is engaged in a never-ending pursuit of the male," said Dare. "Perhaps that explains it."

"Sort o' chase me Charlie," said Bindle, "well I ain't nothink to say agin' it, so long as Mrs. B. don't get to know.

"This place looks like a pub," Bindle remarked a few minutes later. "Wonder wot Mrs. B.'ll say."

"That's what you ought to have, J.B.," said Jim Colman.

"'Ave wot?" enquired Bindle.

"A pub.," was the response.

"I'd like to 'ave a little pub. o' me own," Bindle murmured, "an' I got a name for it too."

In response to loud cries of "Name, name" from the "Tims" men Bindle replied.

"I didn't ought to tell yer, I'm afraid as it's jest like salt, it makes yer drink like a camel."

"Come on out with it," we cried.

"Well, 'ere goes. I'd call it 'The Thirsty Soul.'" After a pause, he added, "If I was in the bung line I'd 'ave the tastiest things in yaller 'eaded gals be'ind the bar as could be found for a 'undred miles round. Of course I should 'ave to get rid o' Mrs. B. first. She's as jealous as an 'en over a china egg wot it ain't laid.

"It's no use bein' in the public line when you're married. Poor ole Artie Ball found that out, 'im wot used to keep 'The Feathers.' One day 'e took 'is barmaid out, an' next mornin' 'is missus took it out o' the barmaid— in 'andfulls, she did. The poor gall looked like an 'alf plucked goose when Artie's missus remembered it was nearly dinner time. Funny thing 'ow women fight over us," this with an air.

A hot argument had sprung up between some of the men from "Tim's" as to the possibility of balancing the human body in the same way that the ancients balanced the figure of Mercury, viz. on one foot, the body thrown forward. This had resulted in a determination of the ayes to prove it by demonstrating the possibility of standing upon a beer bottle with one foot. Soon the infection spread throughout the room, and everybody, with the exception of Sallie, Angell Herald and Bindle, was endeavouring to emulate the classical figure of Eros on the fountain at Piccadilly Circus.

Everybody seemed to be calling upon everybody else to look, and just as they looked, down came the demonstrator. It was this moment that an unkind fate chose for the appearance of Mrs. Bindle. To some extent she had been prepared for the unusual by the line of taxi-cabs in Fenton Street, and also by the tales of the neighbours, who had gathered in ever increasing force. Two local special constables, who had endeavoured to "regulate the traffic" and control the crowds, had given up the task in despair, discovering that no special is a prophet in his own district. One was a butcher, who found it utterly impossible to preserve his official dignity in the face of cries of "Meat! Meat!" and "Buy! Buy!"

By the time Mrs. Bindle arrived, the police-raid theory was in danger of suffering eclipse in favour of a German spy, the nine taxis, it was alleged, having brought soldiers and officials from the War Office.

Mrs. Bindle entered her own home in a state of bewilderment. For a moment or two she stood at the door unseen, endeavouring to penetrate the grey smoke, which was rapidly choking Sallie. Windover was the first to catch sight of her, and he descended hurriedly from his bottle. Then Sallie saw her and next Bindle. Soon the whole room had its eyes fixed upon Mrs. Bindle's attenuated figure, which stood there like an accusing conscience. Bindle grinned, the rest of us looked extremely sheepish, as if caught at something of which we were ashamed. Once more it was Sallie who saved the situation.

"Oh, Mrs. Bindle," she said, going across the room, "I hope you'll forgive us. We heard that Mr. Bindle was ill and came over to see him. I wish you would keep these boys in order." She looked at the "Tim's" men with a smile. "They are always playing tricks of some sort or other."

Mrs. Bindle looked round the room as if uncertain what to do or say. Then her gaze returned to Sallie. We looked at her anxiously to see which way the wind was likely to blow. We almost cheered when we saw a frosty smile flit across her features.

"I'm sure it's very kind of you, miss. Won't you come into the parlour?"

With Mrs. Bindle, "Won't you come into the parlour?" was an announcement of friendship, and Bindle heaved a sigh of relief. Sallie beckoned to Jack Carruthers.

"Jack," she said, "Get those boys to clear up."

Without waiting for Jack to deliver her instructions, everyone set to work to clear up the chaos, and in three minutes the place was as orderly as it had been before our arrival, save for a pile of glasses and mugs in the sink. The bottles had been stowed away in the suit-cases, and the kitchen looked as it did before the descent upon it of the Night Club. Mrs. Bindle had fixed her eyes on the bunch of roses, looted from Dick Little's flat.

"Oh, I brought those for you, Mrs. Bindle," said Sallie.

That broke down Mrs. Bindle's last defences. At Windover's invitation, and in spite of Mrs. Bindle's protests, several of the Tims men set to work to wash up at the sink. Windover did the washing, whilst the others wiped, amidst a perfect babel.

Mrs. Bindle looked from one to the other. Presently turning to Sallie she asked in a whisper, "Is the lord here, miss?"

"The lord?" questioned Sallie in surprise.

"Bindle says a lord belongs to your club. Is he here, miss?"

"Oh! Lord Windover," cried Sallie laughing, "Yes, he's here."

"Is that him, miss?" enquired Mrs. Bindle gazing at Angell Herald, who stood apart from the others with an awkward air of detachment.

Sallie shuddered as she followed Mrs. Bindle's gaze and saw the white satin tie threaded through a diamond ring.

"No, that's Mr. Herald. Lord Windover's washing up. Winnie," she called out, "I want to introduce you to Mrs. Bindle."

Windover approached, eyeglass in eye, with a jug in one hand, a towel he had snatched up in the other, and a red bordered cloth round his waist.

Sallie introduced him and he bowed with his usual exquisite grace, chatted for a few moments, and then returned to his duties at the sink.

In Mrs. Bindle's eyes there was a great wonder, and as they returned to Angell Herald, a little disappointment and regret.

Finally we all trooped off the best of friends. Bindle declared that he was cured, and Mrs. Bindle said she was very pleased that she had come in before we had taken our departure. We stowed ourselves away in the taxis and, as the procession started, Fenton Street raised its voice in a valedictory cheer.

"Winnie," said Sallie to Windover as we bowled eastward at a penny a furlong, "To-night you have wrecked Mrs. Bindle's cherished ideal of the aristocracy. I shall never forget her face when I told her that the man who was washing up was the lord! She had fixed upon Mr. Herald."

Windover screwed his glass into his eye and gazed at Sallie in silence.

Thus ended one of the most notable nights in the history of the Night Club.

CHAPTER XI
THE GENERAL BECOMES A MEMBER

On the Monday morning following our visit to Bindle, Dick Little had descended to General Burdett-Coombe's flat to make a formal apology. The old boy had laughed off the incident as of no importance, refused to allow Dick Little to pay for the damage, and vowed that he liked young fellows with a spice of the devil in them, had been young himself once. He gave his guest a glass of Trafalgar brandy, and had readily accepted an invitation to be present at next Sunday's gathering.

"Damme, sir, I think it will be safer up there than down here," he said as he gazed ruefully up at the ceiling from which hung the wreck of his electrolier.

From that time the General became one of our most regular members, and was well in the first flight as regards popularity. He proved a splendid old fellow, full of good stories of his campaigning experiences, modest and kindly, for all his gust of anger on the night of our first meeting.

From the first he was Sallie's slave. One night he was raving to half-a-dozen of us about Sallie's eyes. "Such eyes," he cried, looking from one to the other as if challenging contradiction, "I never could resist grey eyes. Why damme, sir, if I'd married a girl with grey eyes (the General is a bachelor) I should have been as harmless as— as— — "

"A taube, sir," suggested the Boy slyly.

The General turned on him like a cyclone.

"When I was your age, sir, I should have been shot for interrupting a— — " Then the Boy smiled that radiant, disarming smile of his and the General made a grab at him and missed.

"Wot's a 'towber,' sir?" Bindle enquired of Windover in a whisper. Bindle's whispers are as clearly heard as those of the villain in a melodrama.

"Before the war, J.B.," replied Windover, "'taube' was the German for 'dove'; since then it has become the vehicle of frightfulness."

Bindle looked from Windover to Dare with wrinkled forehead.

"Stripped of its corrosive verbiage, Windover means that 'taube' is the name of a German aeroplane."

"Oh! a tawb," said Bindle, his face clearing. "'E do love to wrap things up, don't 'e?" he added, indicating Windover with an ever-ready thumb. "Anyone could see 'e ain't married."

Later in the evening I heard the Boy say to the General in what he meant to be a whisper—

"I hope I didn't offend you, sir. I ought not to have said— — "

"Tut, tut," said the General. "It's all right, Boy. Damme; but times have changed since I was a youngster," and he pinched the Boy's arm affectionately.

Upon the subject of the new armies the General was particularly interesting. It was easy to see that, coming from army stock, he found the civilian soldier difficult to reconcile with military tradition; but he was a sportsman above all things.

"My Gad! sir," he had exclaimed to a few of us one evening some days after his return from France, where he had been in an official capacity, "they're wonderful. I was prejudiced, I confess it. Imagine an army of stockbrokers, lawyers, fiddlers, clerks and chauffeurs. What could they know of soldiering? But when I saw them, talked with them, why damme, sir, they made me feel a child at the game."

"Keen!" he exclaimed in answer to a question. Then he laughed, "Why there was one young lieutenant-colonel who started as a private two years ago, a splendid officer, and he actually told me that he hated soldiering, hated it, sir, yet was carrying-on as if he cared for nothing else. It's amazing!

"In my time," and the old boy straightened himself to his full five feet nine inches, "the prospect of war sent us half wild with excitement; but these fellows don't like it, have no enthusiasm, want to get back to their pens and tennis-rackets; yet they're born soldiers.

"They talk about funk and feeling afraid in a way that would have got a man ragged out of his regiment in my day;— — Damme, I don't understand it!"

"So you don't altogether disapprove of the new army, General?" It was Sallie who enquired. She had just entered unobserved.

"Disapprove!" cried the General spinning round and shaking hands. "Disapprove! It's a privilege for an old fogey like me to be allowed to talk to such fellows."

"General," said Sallie quietly, "I think the chivalry of the old army is equal to the spirit of the new," and the General actually blushed, at least the red-brown of his cheeks took on a bluish tinge.

When the time came for the General's story I was embarrassed by the choice he offered. There were yarns about every quarter of the globe, and half the races of the earth. Wherever there had been a chance of a brush, the old boy had managed to get sent somewhere close at hand, and when the smoke had burst into flame, he invariably discovered that a month or two's leave was due to him. All his leave seemed to be spent in getting attached to someone else's expeditionary force. Reading between the lines it was easy to see that he was a good officer, and he never seemed to find much difficulty in getting a staff appointment.

<h1 style="text-align:center">I</h1>

It was one of those Indian Frontier affairs of which the world hears little. In high quarters there is a vague consciousness that something has happened, a paragraph or two in the newspapers, with a list of casualties, announces the return of the heroes, a few families are plunged into mourning and there the matter ends.

An expeditionary force was trailing its sinuous, sensitive body wearily along upon the homeward march. The officers were gloomy and short of speech, the men sullen and dispirited. In the hearts of all there was a glow of dull resentment. They had not suffered defeat it is true; still no crushing blow had been struck, and to-day as they toiled silently along in a cloud of dust there was dissatisfaction, a smouldering passion of discontent.

Brigadier-General Charles Stanley de Winton Mossop, C.B., was a man of theories, and the soldier understands theories in direct ratio to their successful application. He is a cog in the great machine of war, and is content if the whole mechanism work smoothly. If he be conscious of any friction of the parts, he unhesitatingly condemns the engineer.

Two months previously, some five thousand men of all arms, had set out elated at the prospect of active service. Even the old campaigners were cynically jovial as they told the "recruities" what to expect. "You wait, sonnies," Sergeant Tonks, a weather-beaten old veteran of twenty years' service, had said good-humouredly, "You just wait, you'll see!" They had seen! They had seen two months of soldiering under service conditions with nothing to show for it, and their ideas of applied war had undergone considerable revision.

They had seen two months of arduous campaigning against a foe that had never learned the meaning of defeat; had never retired or broken but to come again. A foe that sniped all night, and hung about the flanks all day; now showing itself ahead; not threatening the rear, with a special eye for a rush at awkward moments. Striking camp had become a positive torture, and the hour before dawn a period of imaginative suspense; for the men's confidence had been shaken.

At first the subalterns had talked sagely about "protection on the line of march," scouting and the value of "cover." They had views, and a healthy competition had sprung up amongst those in charge of scouting-parties and "flank guards." They had worked with an almost incredible zeal. Every likely bit of "cover" was not only carefully examined, but examined with enthusiasm, even if it were no larger than a man's head. There had been innumerable false alarms, which demonstrated clearly their watchfulness. But that was now a memory. The natural eagerness to excel had been damped, and there had insidiously crept into the minds of all the suspicion that they were badly led.

Brigadier-General Mossop had evolved what was then an entirely new and original conception of the art of war. The present command gave him an opportunity of putting into practice his pet scheme of communicating orders, in the event of night attack, by coloured fires and rockets. He had lectured his officers upon the impossibility of conveying commands accurately by word of mouth in the darkness and confusion of a night attack. Incidentally he had pointed out the advantages of his own method. They had listened respectfully, received his written "Orders of Night Attack" in grim silence, and among themselves had dubbed their commander "Old Brock"; and "Old Brock" he remained to the end.

There was one young subaltern, inclined to regard soldiering as a subject for serious study, who regarded Old Brock's craze for novelty as a grave danger. In a perimeter camp of 5,000 men, rocket communication was, to his view, ridiculous. It might, he argued, at any moment involve the force in disaster. He cast many speculative glances at the chest in which the fireworks were carefully arranged in compartments, each numbered with embossed figures, enabling them to be felt in the dark.

For days the young subaltern went his way wrapped in his own gloom. At length the clouds seemed to disappear as if by magic, and it was noted that he was very frequently seen with the sergeant who had charge of Old Brock's chest.

After a week's march, the force was well into the enemy's country. One dark night a nervous sentry had fired his rifle and explained the circumstance by an account of shadowy forms. Voices barked out peremptory commands, men clutched their rifles and formed up, maxims were cleared and everything made ready. Presently a rocket rose with a majestic whirr and broke into a hundred green stars.

"Old Brock's at it," murmured Major O'Malley.

"That's PREPARE TO RECEIVE ENEMY," murmured a subaltern, who had given much time to the study of his Chief's "Orders."

"Rather late in the day to prepare," growled a captain of gunners. "Might as well say 'Prepare to cut your teeth.'"

The men stood silent, some with a grin of expectation as they gazed in the direction of the Brigadier's tent; others with a queer shivery feeling at the base of the spine, which communicated itself to the knees and teeth. The butt-end of a rifle struck the ground with a dry, hard snap. "Silence!" barked a voice. There was a murmur of deep expostulation, passionate but repressed.

Then a curious thing happened. First a Roman candle vomited its coloured balls into the inky night, casting a ghostly green light upon the upturned faces.

"ENEMY BREAKING THROUGH TO THE EAST. My God!" gasped the subaltern.

There was a movement among the men, and a splutter of rifle-fire which soon died away.

"As you were," shouted a voice. A moment's silence. Next there rose three red and blue rockets, then a swarm of whirring, hissing, serpent-like streams of fire, lighting up the whole encampment as they broke into a thousand points of fire.

It had been the Brigadier's theory to fire the rockets at an angle so as to light up the surrounding country whilst leaving the encampment in darkness. There was a laugh from the ranks, a short, sharp, snapping sound that died almost with its own utterance. More rockets followed, then a red fire gradually sprang into being, dull at first; but growing in volume until eventually it embraced in its ruddy glow the whole country for half a mile round.

"There ain't much fun in watchin' fireworks when yer can't say wot yer think o' them," grumbled one man in a whisper to his neighbour.

The subaltern was busily engaged in trying to read the "Orders of Night Attack." He muttered brokenly from time to time. "ENEMY REPULSED NORTH.— -WITHDRAW TO INNER DEFENCES.— SQUARE BROKEN TO WEST— FIX BAYONETS."— He ceased, and only the crackle of bursting rockets broke the stillness. The red fire began to wane, the rockets ceased, and the darkness became more pronounced. Later, no enemy being discovered, the guards were re-posted and the camp reassumed its normal appearance.

How it happened that the new code of signalling went wrong was never satisfactorily explained. The Brigadier was furious, and next day subjected Sergeant "Rockets," as he was ever afterwards called among the men, to a searching examination. The sergeant could never be persuaded to give an explanation of how it occurred, or what took place afterwards in the Brigadier's tent. There was a story current to the effect that "Rockets" had deliberately brought about the fiasco as a protest against innovation; but the currency of camp-stories is no index to their accuracy.

Three days later an attack upon the camp at dawn had been repulsed with loss; but it had not been followed up. The men chafed and murmured among themselves; the officers saw a golden opportunity for a decisive blow pass unnoticed. "Old Brock," who alone seemed tranquil, penned lengthy dispatches descriptive of the enemy's defeat and discouragement.

So matters went on. Nothing more was accomplished beyond a few successful skirmishes, which to the Brigadier appeared in the light of important victories. The correspondents, there were three, chafed and fretted.

"It's a damned shame," remarked Chisholme hotly, "that the men's hearts should be shrivelled up by such an example of official incapacity. There'll be more heard of this when I get near the telegraph," he added significantly. "You chaps shall get your own back, or* The Morning Independent* is a pulseless, chicken-hearted rag."

Chisholme's directness and picturesque phraseology were proverbial. On this occasion his remarks were directed at Major Blaisby and another officer lounging about the correspondent's tent.

Chisholme had an influential family behind him and this, coupled with the high value he placed upon his own opinions, assured his two friends that, sooner or later, there would be the devil to pay, and the knowledge comforted them. In spite of his insufferable habit of bragging, Chisholme was popular. Strictly speaking he was a non-combatant; yet he had already had several opportunities of showing his mettle. On one occasion at least he had performed an action which, had he been in the Service, would have assured him of the V.C.

Between Correspondent and General a coolness had sprung up. Once the Brigadier had taken occasion to rebuke him for his recklessness, urging as a reason for the remonstrance the possibility of some portion of the force being involved in a disaster, owing to his precipitancy and lack of judgment.

Now that the — — Punitive Expedition was upon the homeward march. The casualties among mules had been extremely heavy, even for a frontier force, and the Brigadier was faced with a grave problem. At a spot about four days' march from the frontier, he announced his intention of establishing a temporary post to guard the sick, the guns and the surplus ammunition. It was a risky proceeding; but the force was running short of food, and must make forced marches to the frontier.

A day was spent in throwing up hasty defenses ("Ruddy scratches," Sergeant Tonks called them), a day spent in active speculation as to who would be selected for the command.

When Major Blaisby of the — th Gurkhas was informed that the Brigadier's choice had fallen upon him, he flushed with pleasure: but when he heard that only fifty men were to be left with him he almost gasped with astonishment. The news spread with the rapidity peculiar to camps, and Blaisby was the centre of a group of brother officers eager in their congratulations, and fervid in their denunciations of the insufficiency of the force.

Blaisby and Chisholme had been on intimate terms, in fact a warm friendship had sprung up between the two men. Immediately on hearing the news, Chisholme had marched straight to the Brigadier's tent and requested to be allowed to remain behind as a volunteer. He met with a curt refusal.

That night, those who were collected in the correspondent's tent, were treated to a remarkable display of eloquence. Chisholme, with his back to the tent-pole, poured forth a burning stream of protest at not being allowed to stay.

Blaisby stood by moody and silent. At length he was persuaded by his impulsive friend to seek out the Brigadier and ask for a larger force. He left with unwilling steps.

In the midst of a particularly eloquent passage on the part of Chisholme, Blaisby returned. He was white to the lips, and there was an ominous quiver about the corners of his mouth. A dead silence greeted him. Then it was that Chisholme showed himself to be something more than an orator. Walking up to Blaisby he linked his arm in his, and led him out of the tent. When he returned alone the Correspondent's tent was empty. There is a fine sense of chivalry among English gentlemen.

Two hours later Chisholme made his way through the darkness to Blaisby's tent. The two men paced up and down conversing earnestly in undertones. The soft light of the false dawn was touching the

Eastern horizon before they parted. Chisholme returned to his tent and threw himself down to snatch an hour's sleep. Blaisby continued to pace up and down until the light grew stronger, when he fetched a small portmanteau from his tent, and at this improvised table he sat writing letters until reveille sounded.

As soon as the Brigadier was stirring his orderly informed him that Lieutenant Blaisby wished to know when it would be convenient to see him. The Brigadier, suppressing an exclamation of impatience, bade the orderly shew him in. For half-an-hour the two remained together. Finally Blaisby left the tent with a grim, set face and went to seek Chisholme.

The sun was well up when the march was resumed. As the main body got into motion the men broke out into "Auld Lang Syne." The Brigadier sent an A.D.C. to "stop that damned folly." There was a wringing of hands as his comrades bade farewell to Blaisby. Three hearty cheers split the air, bringing a frown to the Brigadier's face. He said nothing, feeling that the men were none too well in hand. As he rode along by the side of his Brigade-Major he surprised that officer by remarking "Blaisby is a very able officer,— we shall hear more of him."

Chisholme remained behind until the rearguard was almost out of sight, then with a hasty handshake and a "God bless you, old chap" he galloped off.

Blaisby now found himself with thirty-five native and fifteen white troops, two subalterns and a young surgeon, in all fifty-three. He walked round the hastily formed entrenchment and viewed the whole with a calm impassive face. Turning to the senior sub. he bade him call the men together. In a few words he told them that they were upon a very dangerous service. The work would be arduous and the fighting hard, but they must remember that their own safety and the honour of the corps from which they were drawn depended upon their exertions. The men cheered, and the eyes of the little Gurkhas flashed at the thought of handgrips with the enemy.

Directly the mid-day meal was over, the force was divided into three parties: one was sent out scouting, another ordered to sleep, whilst the third, under Blaisby himself, set to work with pick and spade.

For two days and nights they worked without cessation: entrenching, scouting, sleeping; sleeping, entrenching, scouting. "Blaisby'll be a corpse or a colonel before the year's out," remarked the junior sub. At first the men worked doggedly, as well-trained soldiers will. They were taking the measure of their commander, watching him furtively whilst on duty, discussing him eagerly over their pipes when relieved. Soon they began to fall under the spell of his personality, and a wave of enthusiasm took possession of them. The private is ever ready to acknowledge a master mind, and next to knowing that his officer is a gentleman, he likes best to feel that he is a being of superior attainments.

At the end of two days, a formidable array of defences had been completed. In the centre a pit, some six feet deep and thirty feet square, had been dug. This was roofed over with canvas. A cutting three feet wide gave entrance to "the oven," as it came to be called, which was to act as arsenal and hospital for the worst cases. The guns and much of the surplus ammunition were built into the camp-defences.

Everything now being ready, the men were ordered to rest. Never did men sleep so in the history of war. They were sick of sleep; yet Blaisby's personality had taken such a grip of their minds, that eyes would close mechanically at his approach. He wished them to sleep; they would sleep if it killed them.

One night Blaisby happened to overhear a remark of the surgeon. "It's all very well to say sleep," he grumbled, "But how the devil is a man to sleep unless he's tired?" The next day orders were given to keep the men occupied with sports. Running, jumping, wrestling, skipping, sparring and every conceivable form of exercise was indulged in. Blaisby gave prizes in money, until his small store was exhausted, then he turned to his kit and distributed all he could actually spare as prizes. The men were thus kept interested and occupied.

On the third day after the departure of the main body the enemy was sighted; why they had not attacked at once was never explained. The next day a movement was observed upon some rising ground, to the eastward. Forms were observed flitting about, tiny dots of white relieved here and there by a splash of brilliant green, as a banner caught the rays of the setting sun. That night a keener watch than ever was kept.

An hour before dawn, a rifle shot snapped out sharply upon the crisp night air. Absolute silence reigned. Presently a sharp challenge rang out, followed by a shot and a yell, then a trailing splutter of reports, then silence again. The enemy drew off on finding everything ready for his reception.

After this the little garrison knew no repose. Attack followed attack, and seldom a night passed without an alarm. It was evidently the object of the enemy to wear out the defenders with constant watching. On one occasion they almost rushed the defences, and were repulsed only at the point of the bayonet. Blaisby grew grave as he saw the casualties increase. The suspense and frequent alarms began to tell their tale. The men were worn out, and although they slept whenever opportunity offered during the day, it was always with the possibility of being awakened to repel an attack.

Each night Blaisby spent upon the look-out platform, and was frequently to be seen at dawn scanning the horizon to the south through his field-glasses.

One evening, after a more than usually spirited attack by the enemy, Blaisby sat silent at the table, whilst the senior sub. and the surgeon talked over the day's work. They had been puzzled at the action of their commander after the repulse. He had selected ten of the Gurkhas and taken them into the "Oven," posting a sentry at the entrance and had remained there with the junior sub. until dinner-time. The senior sub. and the surgeon were piqued at not being confided in.

The surgeon had just finished a lengthy harangue upon the methods it was desirable to adopt in savage warfare, ridiculing the textbooks as academic. As he concluded he raised his eyes from their gloomy contemplation of the end of his cigar. They became fixed, his jaw dropped. The senior sub. half-turned to see the cause. He uttered an exclamation! At the entrance of the tent stood a grim and ghastly figure, with rolling eyes and grinning lips. The two men stared as if bewitched at what appeared to be a reincarnation of Beelzebub. The apparition remained motionless save for the movement of its eyes, hideous, unearthly eyes, encircled with rings of red and surmounted by white brows. Then there was the great red mouth and the diabolical black horns which sprang suddenly from snowy hair.

Every bone in the dusky body was outlined in white. The two men turned almost appealingly to Blaisby, who sat impassively watching them.

"Sorry to startle you; it's an experiment," he said as he made a motion with his hand at which the figure disappeared, "upon men whose minds are trained against superstition."

That was all. He rose and went out, leaving the surgeon and senior sub. speechless and indignant. At midnight eleven ghostly figures emerged from the "Oven" and slid away into the darkness. Shortly afterwards Blaisby mounted to the look-out platform where he stood silent and immovable, his gaze directed eastward.

II

Whilst Blaisby and his men were busily occupied with the defense of "Old Brock's Folly," the main body of the Expeditionary Force had reached the frontier. The Brigadier appeared uncertain how to act. The officers were moody, and the men silent, almost sullen. Orders were obeyed without alacrity, without zeal, without cheerfulness.

Two days passed without any preparations for the relief of the "Post." At length with a rather over-done careless air the Brigadier remarked to his Senior Colonel upon the spiritlessness of the troops after a "victorious campaign." The Senior Colonel made an equally casual rejoinder. The men were tired, he had frequently noticed a similar state of affairs at the end of an expedition. There the matter had ended for the moment. Later a further remark from the Brigadier had met with a like evasion on the part of his subordinate.

That Brigadier-General Mossop's nerves were disordered was plainly shown by his lack of decision. Orders were given and countermanded; elaborate dispatches were penned, only to be destroyed an hour later. At last the Senior Colonel was startled by a point blank request for his opinion as to the advisability of despatching a force to relieve the post without waiting for further supplies.

A decisive, "I consider it highly expedient, sir, if not too late," was not reassuring.

For two days the Brigadier pondered over the significant words. "If not too late." He saw the possibility of the dreaded official reprimand. At length the order was given: a third of the force was to retrace its steps and relieve the little garrison, "If not too late," the words obtruded themselves upon the Brigadier's mind and irritated him.

Thus it happened that, after days of inactivity and indecision, the Relief Force set out under the command of the Senior Colonel. As it swung off to the brisk notes of the bugle, spirits rose as if by magic, jokes were cracked amongst the rank and file, the old jokes that yesterday would have fallen flat now drew a hearty laugh. All were elated at the prospect of a brush with the enemy. This was to be a fight to the finish. The Senior Colonel was a soldier of a different type from the Brigadier. He had no theories, as theories are generally understood. His dictum was to fight— and win. If there were heavy casualties, he deplored it as a necessary feature of his profession. The men knew this— there would be hard knocks and they thanked God for it.

Shortly before sunset on the third day, the force halted behind some rising ground about four miles south-east of the "Post." The enemy had been located and the Senior Colonel was not the man to wait. He had resolved to push on and risk a night attack. Half the column was to make a detour and approach from the north-east, whilst the other half attacked from the eastward. After a hasty meal and a short rest, the first party moved off guided by the stars and a compass. Silently it disappeared into the darkness. An hour later the other half set out.

Chisholme, who had managed to be included, was well ahead with the advance guard of the first column. After an hour's steady marching to the eastward they bore round to the north and later swung round to the south-west. Half an hour passed and the scouts brought in word that the enemy's camp lay about a mile ahead, a little to the westward of the line of march. Presently the advance guard halted to allow the main body to come up. The order came to continue the advance "with great caution."

Scarcely were they in motion again before a point of red fire caught Chisholme's eye, followed by several similar lights. Wild yells broke the stillness, more lights followed until the whole encampment was bathed in a blood-red glow. Through his night-glasses, Chisholme saw a veritable pandemonium. Dancing forms— eerie, horrible, devilish— moved rhythmically to and fro, each the centre of a sphere of hellish light. Was it some nightmare of the Infernal Regions? Could he be dreaming? He looked round. Officers and men were gazing wonder-struck.

The noise was fiendish: hoarse shouts, shrill cries, terror-stricken yells split the air. Gradually the glow increased in volume. Wild forms were seen silhouetted sharply against the light, rushing hither and thither in a frenzy of terror. Slowly the strange figures approached the camp: dancing and swaying, without hurry, without excitement. Chisholme rubbed his eyes, then looking again beheld a wild mob of fleeing tribesmen coming straight towards him, bent only on escaping from the furies.

A few short, sharp orders rang out. A moment later the crackle of rifles drowned the cries. A machine-gun began to stutter and spit. The terrified tribesmen paused stunned and dropped in dozens. Firing was heard to the southward— the others were at it also.

At this moment the advance was sounded. The main force had come up, deployed and with a yell rushed forward to the charge. A portion of the enemy broke away to the north; but the majority stood transfixed with terror. Some threw themselves upon the bayonets, others stood impassively awaiting death. A few who had weapons showed fight; but were soon cut down.

A couple of rockets rose to the westward.

"Thank God," muttered the Senior Colonel, "we're in time." The work of slaughter continued grimly, silently: short sobbing coughs were heard as the cold steel found its mark.

Presently the recall was sounded. The men were becoming scattered and the Senior Colonel was troubled about those queer figures still to be seen gathered round the fire. Collecting a few men together, he advanced. As he approached, the forms started whirling and dancing, the coloured fires burst out again and the astonished officer saw eleven careering forms, skeletons apparently, with white hair and black horns.

"Well, I'm damned!" he gasped.

"And Hell within jumping distance," muttered a voice.

"Who goes there?" rang out the challenge apparently from the tallest devil.

"Friend," was the reply.

"Advance and give the countersign."

"Who the devil are you?" burst out the Senior Colonel.

"Servants of Her Britannic Majesty, Queen Victoria."

With shouts and laughter officers and men alike rushed forward, and there was a babel of congratulatory voices.

III

Dawn was breaking when Major Blaisby finished his account of what had happened during those four eventful weeks. "It was Chisholme's idea," he concluded, "that I should ask the Brigadier for the fireworks in order to give his system an extended trial." He did not add that the object of the request was to placate his superior, in order to obtain the maxim.

When the light became stronger, the Senior Colonel examined the defences, and complimented Blaisby in his short, gruff manner. "You've made a fine show, Blaisby," he said in conclusion, "A damned sight finer show than I should have made."

Chisholme had his opportunity later, when THE MORNING INDEPENDENT printed a series of brilliantly written articles upon the campaign and its ending, and although more moderate in tone than many expected, Brigadier General Mossop saw in those articles the explanation of his receiving no official mark of approval for the way in which he had conducted the − − Punitive Expedition.

"An' where did you come in, sir?" enquired Bindle of the General, when he had finished "leading the applause" with his mallet.

"I?" said the General, "What do you mean?"

"Well, sir, I wondered if by any chance it was you wot mixed the fireworks so as they all went off wrong."

The General laughed. Sallie said the General was at his best when a laugh caused his teeth to flash white against the surrounding tan.

"A shrewd guess, by jove," he exclaimed, "Yes, it was I who mixed the fireworks."

"And what would you do sir now if a sub., under your command, were to do the same," enquired the Boy languidly.

"Confound you sir, if it were you I'd have you shot," he shouted. Somehow the General seemed always to shout at the Boy.

"No, you wouldn't, General," said Sallie, giving the poor old boy a sidelong glance that temporarily threw him off his balance.

"And why, may I ask?"

"Because I should ask you to let him off."

"Then," said the General with decision, "I should deserve to be shot.

"An' is that Major alive now, sir?" queried Bindle.

"Who, Blaisby? Yes," replied the General; "but that's not his name. If I were to tell you who he is and what he is doing to-day, you'd understand the awful risk the country ran through the Commander-in-Chief of India giving commands to rabbits instead of soldiers."

"I'm glad he got through," said Sallie meditatively.

"You can never keep a good man back," remarked the General in that modified tone of voice he always adopted when speaking to Sallie.

"Wot's 'e goin' to do if 'e's got various veins in 'is legs, I wonder?" I heard Bindle mutter as he knocked the ashes out of his pipe.

CHAPTER XII
THE MATER

Except when "roasting" Angell Herald, the Boy is not much given to speech. Humped up in the easiest chair available, he will sit apparently absorbed in the contemplation of his well-polished finger-nails, or preoccupied with the shapeliness of his shoes and the silkiness of his socks; yet his mind is keenly alert, as some of us occasionally discover to our cost. A sudden laugh from those about him will demonstrate that the Boy is awake and has scored a point, more often than not at Angell Herald's expense.

There is something restful and refreshing in the fugitive smile that seems to flicker across the Boy's face when, by accident, you catch his eye. He is one of those intensely lovable and sympathetic beings who seem constitutionally incapable of making enemies. As mischievous as a puppy, he would regard it as an "awful rag" to hide a man's trousers when he is late for parade. Then he would be "most frightfully sorry" afterwards— and really mean it.

We all became much attached to him, and looked forward with concern to the time when he would be drafted out to the front again. After the Loos battle he had been attached to the depot of the Westshires at Wimbledon. From Windover we learned a great deal about the Boy, who seemed possessed of one unassailable conviction and one dominating weakness. The conviction was that he was "a most awful ass" and "rather a rotter": the weakness was "the Mater." He seldom spoke of her, but when he did a softness would creep into his voice, and his eyes would lose their customary look of amused indolence.

Mrs. Summers was something of an invalid, and whenever he could the Boy would spend hours in wheeling her bath-chair about Kensington Gardens and Hyde Park, or sitting with her at home playing "Patience." This he would do, not from a sense of duty; but because of the pleasure it gave him.

He seemed to go through life looking for things that would interest or amuse "the Mater." From France he sent a stream of things, from aluminium rings to a German machine-gun. There had been some trouble with the Authorities over the machine-gun, which had been put on board a French train and the carriage heavily prepaid. The thing had been held up and enquiries instituted, which had resulted in the Boy paying a visit to the orderly-room to explain to his C.O. what he meant by trying to send Government property to S. Kensington.

"But, sir, we took it, and the men didn't want it," the Boy explained ingenuously.

"Boy," said the Colonel, "In war there is only one thing personal to the soldier, and that is his identity disc."

"I'm most awfully sorry, sir," said the Boy with heightened colour.

"Now look here Boy," said the Colonel, "If by chance you happen to capture a battery of howitzers, I must beg of you for the honour of the regiment not to send them home. Look at that!" He indicated a sheaf of official-looking papers lying on the table before him. Between Whitehall and G.H.Q. an almost hysterical exchange of official memoranda had taken place.

"These are the results of your trying to send a German machine-gun to your mother," and in spite of himself the Colonel's eyes smiled, and the Boy saluted and withdrew. There the incident had ended, that is officially; but out of it, however, grew a tradition. Whenever the 8th Westshires captured anything particularly unwieldy, the standing joke among the men was, "Better post it to the Kid's mother."

One day an enormously fat German prisoner was marched up to the Field Post Office labelled for the Boy's mother. The Bosche, a good-humoured fellow, appeared to enter heartily into the joke, not so the post-office orderly, who threatened to report the post-corporal who had tendered the "packet."

The morning following the taking of the B— — n Farm after a desperate fight, the Senior Major, then in command, was surprised to see an enormous piece of cardboard fashioned in the shape of a label, attached to the wall. addressed

```
+ -------------------------------+
| MRS. SOMERS,              |
|     860, Prince's Gate,    |
|         S. Kensington,    |
|             London, S.W.  |
| With love                 |
| from the Kid.             |
+ -------------------------------+
```

Between men of the Westshires and their officers there was complete understanding, and the Senior Major had smiled back at the grinning faces that seemed to spring up all round him. Unfortunately the Divisional Commander, a martinet of the old school who could not assimilate the spirit of the new armies, had tactlessly chosen that afternoon on which to inspect the captured position. He had gazed fiercely at the label, demanding what the devil it meant, and without waiting for a reply, had expressed himself in unequivocal terms upon "damned buffoonery" and "keeping the men in hand." Finally he had strutted off, his cheeks puffed out with indignation. That occurred after the Boy's return to London.

Dick Little possessed an enormous bible with Gustave Doré's illustrations, a strangely incongruous thing for him to own. One evening the Boy dug it out from the chaos of volumes that Dick Little calls his "library." For some time he turned over the leaves industriously. I was puzzled to account for his interest in Doré's impossible heights and unthinkable depths.

That night he staggered off with the Doré's anticipations of eternity under his arm, which he had borrowed from Dick Little. Bindle watched him in obvious surprise.

"'Andy little thing to read when yer strap-'angin' in a toobe," he remarked drily.

"It's a bible," I explained.

"An' wot's Young 'Indenburg want with a bible?" enquired Bindle in surprise.

"You've probably awakened in his young mind a thirst for theology," remarked Dare, who had joined us. But Bindle did not smile. He was clearly puzzled.

On the following Sunday, Bindle tackled the Boy on the subject.

"Why jer go orf wi' that little pocket bible, sir?" he enquired.

The Boy flushed.

"I thought the Mater would like to see it," was the response, and Bindle began to talk about pigeons as if he had not heard.

We had often asked Windover to describe the Boy's mother; but he had always put us off, saying that he could never describe anybody, except the Kaiser, and King Edward had done that before him.*

* Windover was evidently referring to King Edward's remark, "The fellow is not a gentleman."

Sallie was greatly interested in the Boy's devotion to his mother, and she lost no opportunity of drawing him out. At first he was shy and uncommunicative; but when Sallie is set upon extracting anything from a man, S. Anthony himself would have to capitulate.

From the scraps of conversation I overheard, I came to picture a son full of tender solicitude and awkward devotion for a little white-haired lady with a beautiful expression, a gentle voice and a smile that she would leave behind as a legacy to her son.

I could see the old lady's pride at the sight of the red and blue ribbon on the Boy's tunic, at the letter his C.O. had written to the "Old Dad," her thankfulness at his safe return.

We found ourselves wanting to meet this little white-haired old lady with the smile of sunshine, and hear her welcome us in a gentle, but rather tired voice.

She would be interested in the Night Club, concerned if we did not eat of her dainty scones, or would it be shortbread, anxious that we make a long call. There would be glances of meaning and affection exchanged between her and the Boy, which we would strive not to intercept, and feel self-conscious should we by chance do so. Then she would ask us to come again, saying how glad she always was to see her boy's friends.

During the long talks that Sallie had with the Boy, Bindle used to fidget aimlessly about, the picture of discontent. He always became a little restive if Sallie showed too great an interest in the conversation of any man but himself. It was Bindle in a new guise.

One evening the Boy, who arrived late, was greeted by Bindle with,

"'Ullo! sir, you doin' the Romeo stunt? as Mr. Angell 'E rald would say."

"The what, J.B.?" enquired the Boy innocently.

"I see you last Thursday at South Ken. with a bowkay as if you was goin' to a weddin'. 'Ooo's yer lady friend, Mr. 'Indenburg?"

The Boy flushed scarlet.

"Mr. Bindle," said Sallie severely, who has intuitions, "I'm cross with you."

"Wi' me, miss?" Bindle enquired in concerned surprise. "Wot 'ave I done?"

"It's all right," broke in the Boy. "The flowers were for the Mater."

Bindle became strangely silent, for some time afterwards. Later he said to me—

"'E seems fond of 'is mother."

"Who?" I enquired.

"Young 'Indenburg. I'm sorry for wot I said." Then he added meditatively. "If I 'ad a kid I'd like 'im to grow up like 'im," and Bindle jerked his thumb in the direction of where the Boy stood listening to the General's views upon army discipline.

"Mr. Bindle," said Sallie who came up at that moment, having detached herself from Angell Herald's saloon-bar civilities, "I'm going to see Mrs. Somers on Wednesday and I shall tell her about your remark. I think he's a dear."

"I'm sorry, miss," said Bindle with genuine contrition.

"She must be a very wonderful and beautiful old lady to inspire such devotion."

"Oo, miss?"

"The Boy's mother," I murmured.

"I'd like to see 'er," said Bindle seriously, and we knew he meant it.

The Sunday following I asked Sallie about her visit to the Boy's mother, and I was struck at the strangeness of her manner. It was obvious that she did not wish to talk about it. I made several attempts, Bindle also tried; but with equal unsuccess.

If Sallie is determined not to talk about a thing, nothing will drag it out of her, and seeing that she had made up her mind I accordingly desisted. Bindle saw for himself that it would be better to let the matter drop.

"Funny thing 'er not wantin' to say anythink about it," he muttered.

We were both greatly puzzled to account for Sallie's strange behaviour. I noticed that her eyes were often on the Boy, and in them was an expression that I found baffling. Sometimes I thought it was pity, at others tenderness.

It was two weeks later that the mystery was solved. I had invited Bindle to tea in Kensington Gardens, and we had sat rather late bestowing the caterer's cake and biscuits upon birds and gamins. In this Bindle took great delight. The game was to convey a piece of cake, or a biscuit, to a young urchin without being caught in the act by a keen-eyed waitress.

"When she catches yer it's like bein' pinched wi' yer 'and in a bishop's pocket," explained Bindle, which was rather a good description.

After tea we walked slowly through the Gardens. Suddenly Bindle clutched my arm.

"Look, sir! Look!" he cried excitably, pointing to a path that led off at right angles from the walk we were following. "It's Young 'Indenburg."

I saw approaching us the Boy, pushing a bath-chair, the occupant of which was hidden by a black lace sunshade. Instinctively Bindle and I turned down the path, for we knew that in that bath-chair was the beautiful old lady who had given to us the Boy.

Suddenly the Boy looked up and saw us. He stooped down and said something to the occupant of the bath-chair. A second later the position of the black sunshade was altered and— several things seemed to happen all at once. The Boy stopped, came round to the front of the bath-chair and presented us, a strange tenderness alike in his voice and expression as he did so, Bindle dropped his stick and I received a shock.

Where was the beautiful, white-haired old lady, her smiling eyes, the gentle lovable mouth— — ? I shuddered involuntarily, and after a few minutes' exchange of pleasantries, during which I behaved like a schoolboy and Bindle was absolutely dumb, I pleaded a pressing engagement and we made our adieux.

For some minutes we walked on in silence. I seemed to see nothing but that pinched and peevish face, to hear nothing but the querulous, complaining voice.

So that was the Boy's mother. I turned to Bindle, curious to see the effect upon him. I had never before seen him look so serious.

"I'm glad I can't remember my mother," he said, and that seemed to end the matter. We never referred to it again. Somehow it would have seemed disloyal to the Boy. Later in the evening, when the Night Club was in session, the Boy said to me,

"I'm awfully glad you saw us to-day. I wanted you and J.B. to meet the Mater."

There was on his face the same expression and in his voice the same softness I had noticed in the afternoon. I caught Sallie's eye, and I remembered her reticence.

"Then he must get it from the Old Dad after all," I murmured, and Sallie nodded and passed on to a group at the other end of the room.

CHAPTER XIII
THE ROMANCE OF A HORSEWHIPPING

The more I saw of Jocelyn Dare the more I got to like him. Beneath the superficialities of the poseur there was a nature that seemed oddly out of keeping with the twentieth century. He was intended for the days of chivalry and the clashing of spear against breast-plate. To his love of children I have already referred, and with animals he was equally gentle. I once saw him in Piccadilly, immaculately dressed as usual, with his arms round the neck of a bus-horse that had fallen and was in danger of being strangled by the collar.

Dare, Sallie, and Bindle became great friends, and would talk "animals" by the hour together. Bindle would go further than the others, and would discourse with affectionate regret of the "special sort o' performin' fleas" he had once kept. At first Sallie would shrink from these references; but when she saw that Bindle had been genuinely attached to the little creatures, she braced herself up to their occasional entry into the conversation.

"Have you noticed," Angell Herald once whispered to me, "how Bindle's fleas seem to annoy Miss Carruthers?"

The whisper was loud and came during one of those unaccountable hushes in the general talk. In consequence everybody heard. It was an awkward moment, and Angell Herald became the colour of a beetroot.

It was Bindle who saved the situation by saying with regret in his voice: "I lost 'em more'n a year ago, so that can't be."

Dare would often drop in upon me for half an hour's chat. If I were too busy to talk, he would curl himself up in my arm-chair and become as silent as a bird.

One night he was sitting thus when I aroused him from his reverie by banging a stamp on an envelope with an air of finality that told him work was over for that night.

"Finished?" he queried with a smile.

I nodded and lit a cigarette. I was feeling brain-weary and Dare, with that ready sympathy of his which is almost feminine, seemed instinctively to understand that I required my thoughts diverting from the day's work.

"Ever horsewhip a man?" he enquired languidly as he reached for another cigarette.

"No," I replied, scenting a story.

"Well, don't," was the reply.

Dare then proceeded to tell me the story of the one and only horsewhipping in which he had participated. The story came as a godsend, for I had nothing for the next meeting of the Night Club.

I

"If you intended to horsewhip a man, Walters, how would you begin?" enquired Jocelyn Dare of his man one morning at breakfast.

Without so much as the fraction of a second's hesitation Walters placed the omelette before his master, lifted the cover, gave a comprehensive glance at the table to see that nothing was lacking, then in the most natural manner in the world replied, "I should buy a whip, sir."

That was Walters all over. He is as incapable of surprise as water of compression. He is practical to his finger-tips, that is what makes him the most excellent of servants. I have met Walters and I use him when Peake, my own man, evinces the least tendency to slackness. If Dare were to take home an emu or an octopus as a household pet, Walters would, as a matter of course, ring up the Zoological Gardens and enquire as to the most desirable aliment for sustaining life in their respective bodies. To Dare Walters is something between an inspiration and a habit.

"Stop!" cried Dare, as Walters was about to leave the room. "This is a matter of some importance and cannot be so lightly dismissed."

Walters returned to the table, readjusted the toast-rack at its proper angle, and replaced the cover on what remained of the omelette. One of Walters' most remarkable qualities is that, no matter how suddenly he may be approached upon a subject, or how bizarre the subject itself, his reply is always that of a man who has just been occupied in a careful and deliberate analysis of the matter in question from its every conceivable aspect.

"Well, having bought the whip," Dare queried as he took another piece of toast, "how would you then proceed if you wanted to horsewhip a man?"

"I should never want to horsewhip anyone, sir. No one ever does," was the unexpected reply.

Dare looked up at Walters' expressionless face.

"But," said Dare, "I have just told you that I want to horsewhip someone. Will you have it that I am the only man who has ever wanted to horsewhip another?"

"Begging your pardon, sir," said Walters. "But you do not really want to horsewhip anyone."

Dare put down his fork and stared at Walters in interested surprise. After a careful examination of his servant's features he remarked, "I have never disguised from you, Walters, my admiration for your capacity of transmuting eggs into omelettes, your unerring taste in neckwear, your inspiration in trouserings, your knowledge of Burke and your attainments as a compendium of knowledge upon the subtleties of etiquette; but I think you might permit me to know my own feelings in the matter of horsewhipping."

"I beg your pardon, sir," Walters' tone was deferential but firm. "I was with Lord Beaulover when her Ladyship eloped with Mr. Jameson. His Lordship was quite upset about it."

"But what has this got to do with horsewhipping?" questioned Dare.

"I was coming to that, sir," replied Walters evenly. "His Lordship was so kind as to ask my opinion as to what he should do. His Lordship was always very kind in consulting me upon his private affairs."

"And what did you advise?" queried Dare.

"I told him that the correct thing would be to horsewhip Mr. Jameson. His Lordship protested that he was not angry with Mr. Jameson, but as a matter of fact deeply indebted to him. We were speaking in strict confidence, I should mention, sir."

"Of course," said Dare. "Go on, Walters."

"Well, sir, his Lordship eventually agreed that his duty to Society demanded physical violence. He was always most punctilious in— — "

"But I thought it was young Jameson who whipped Lord Beaulover," broke in Dare.

"That is so, sir," replied Walters, "But his Lordship did not on this occasion see the force of my arguments that he should practise beforehand. He was confined to his bed for a week and suffered considerable pain. I remember him saying to me:

" 'Walters, never again.'

" 'No, my Lord,' I replied.

" 'I mean,' continued his Lordship, 'I'll never go against your advice again, Walters, never!'

"And he never did, sir."

"Is that all you have to say upon the ethics of horsewhipping, Walters?" Dare enquired as he proceeded to enjoy the omelette au jambon, in the making of which Walters is an adept.

"It would be advisable to make careful preparation, sir," was Walters' matter-of-fact reply. "There was the mishap of his Lordship."

"Yes," Dare mused as he poured out another cup of coffee; "there's always that danger. Life is crammed with anti-climax."

"Yes, sir!"

"How would you go to work, Walters?" Dare questioned.

Without a moment's hesitation Walters replied, "I do not know, sir, whether you have noticed that even battles now-a-days have to be rehearsed."

"Ah!" broke in Dare, "you advise a répétition générale."

"The chief difficulty, sir," continued Walters, "is to get a good grip of your man. May I ask, sir, who it is you intend to horsewhip?"

Dare looked quickly up at Walters. There was no curiosity in his face, he evidently required the information for the purpose of reaching his conclusions.

"Mr. Standish," Dare replied, watching Walters narrowly to see if he showed surprise. Standish and his wife were at that time Dare's most intimate friends, and they were constantly at his flat and Dare at theirs.

Walters did not move a muscle.

"Mr. Standish has a very thick neck, sir," he remarked, "that makes it more difficult."

Dare put down the coffee cup he was just raising to his lips and stared at Walters.

"What on earth has that to do with it?" he exclaimed.

"It is more difficult to get a good grip of a man with a thick neck, sir, than of one with a thin neck. Fortunately I have a thick neck," he added imperturbably.

Walters has always been a great joy to Dare; but there are times when he is also something of a trial. Dare suggested that he should explain himself, which he proceeded to do.

According to Walters, rehearsal is the great educator. If he were asked his advice as to how to run away with another man's wife, he would insinuate that there must be a sort of dress-rehearsal. His creed is that to a man of the world nothing must appear as a novelty. Breeding, he would define as the faculty of doing anything and everything as if to the action accustomed.

On the matter of horsewhipping, Dare learned much during the next ten minutes, and by the time he had finished his breakfast he found himself in full possession of all the necessary information as to how to horsewhip a man. The thickness of his own neck, Walters appeared to regard as the special provision of providence that his master might practise upon him. Dare protested that it would hurt, and Walters countered with a reference to the pile of old copies of THE TIMES awaiting a call from the Boy Scouts. With these he would pad himself and instruct Dare in how, when and where to horsewhip a fellow being.

But for Walters, Dare confesses, he would have made a sorry mess of that whipping. The whip seemed to get entangled in everything. It brought down pictures, lifted chairs, demolished an electric light bracket, and uprooted a fern. In short it seemed bewitched. Dare could get it anywhere but upon Walters' person. When somewhat more practised, Dare brought off a glorious cut upon Walters' right leg, which set him hopping about the room in silent agony. Greatly concerned Dare apologised profusely.

"It was my own fault, sir," was Walters' reply as he proceeded to bind a small mat round each leg. "I omitted all protection below the knee."

After a week's incessant practice upon Walters' long-suffering body and patient spirit, Dare was given to understand that he might regard himself as having successfully passed out of his noviciate.

When Dare confided to Jack Carruthers what he intended to do, Carruthers burst out with—

"Good heavens! Why, Standish is your best pal and his wife— — "

"Had better be left out of the picture as far as you're concerned, old man," had been the reply. "The modern habit of linking thought to speech irritates me intensely: it shows a deplorable lack of half tones."

Carruthers apologised.

"But why do you want to whip Millie Standish's husband?" Carruthers demanded, pulling vigorously at his pipe, a trick of his when excited.

According to Dare, Carruthers is sometimes hopelessly English, not in his ideas; but in his method of expressing them— his ideas themselves are Continental. Dare told him that by saying Millie Standish's husband, instead of Standish, he implied that he, Dare, was in love with another man's wife.

Carruthers had blurted out that of course he was, everybody knew it.

Dare pointed out that he had got mixed in his tenses. To BE in love with a married woman is apt to compromise her: to HAVE BEEN in love with her, merely adds to her interest and importance in the eyes of her contemporaries.

That is Dare all over. He would stop his own funeral service to point a moral, or launch an epigram.

Standish and Dare had been close friends until Standish fell insanely in love with the young woman who dispensed "tonics" in the saloon-bar of "The Belted Earl." Standish was a bizarre creature at times, and, to use Dare's own words, "what must the braying jackass do but endeavour to cultivate Fay's (that was his inamorata's classic name) mind, which existed nowhere outside the radius of his own mystical imagination."

On her nights out he took her to ballad concerts, when her soul yearned for the Pictures; and to University extension lectures, when her whole being craved for the Oxford.

When she complained of the long hours and the "sinking" she felt between meals, he advised her to eat raisins, and descanted sagely upon the sustaining properties of sugar. No one will ever know how he got acquainted with her, for drink made him either sick or silly. However, every evening between six and seven Standish ran into "The Belted Earl" on his way home, consumed a small lemonade, and handed Fay her morrow's ration of raisins.

He confided the whole story to Dare, he was bursting with it. Dare gave him sage counsel built up upon the foundation of secrecy, but instinctively he knew that it was impossible with a man like Standish.

One night Standish insisted upon Dare accompanying him into the saloon-bar of "The Belted Earl" where he was formally introduced to what Dare described as "a big-busted creature, with a head like a blonde horse and teeth suggestive of a dentist's show-case."

Fay's conversation seemed to consist mainly of three phrases, which are given in the order of the frequency with which they escaped her

1.   Oh! go on, do!
2.   I'm surprised at you!
3.   Aren't you sarcastic!

Standish strove to be light in his talk, possibly with the object of matching his beloved's hair; but, like that peroxide-exotic, his thoughts were rooted in darker foundations.

As they left the place Standish enquired eagerly—

"What do you think of her?"

Dare became deliberately mixed over the pronoun, and replied with a very direct description of what he thought of Standish.

He told him that he was confusing his conception of the soul with Fay's conviction of the body. He scoffed at the concerts and lectures. He pointed out that the politic Fay suffered them because she had imagination. "You are endeavouring to combine the instincts of a lothario with the soul of a calvinist," Dare had said in conclusion.

The two men parted with their friendship considerably shaken. Dare saw no particular objection to Standish making an ass of himself over any girl he chose; but he could not digest the missionary spirit in which Standish chose to view the whole adventure.

At last Standish went a step too far and told his wife all about it, requesting her to ask the unspeakable Fay to call. This platonic request was very naturally refused, and Standish made a fool of himself, said that Fay was one of Nature's ladies, and, given the right clothes and environment, she would be an astonishing success.

Dare learned the story from both of them, and told Standish that such bloods as he were wanted in sparsely populated colonies. The upshot was a breach between the two.

Millie Standish took it all rather badly. She talked about leaving her husband, and there was a quiet determined look in her eyes that Dare did not like: it seemed to suggest the possibility of leaving the world as well. Dare talked about brain-storm and other alien things, and patched things up for the time being.

At last Dare determined that shock tactics were necessary to bring Standish to his senses, and here his chivalry asserted itself. Millie Standish had no brother, therefore Dare felt it incumbent upon him to assume the fraternal responsibility of correcting Standish's rather Eastern views of life.

II

Having become thoroughly practised, Dare waited outside Standish's office one morning and administered the necessary punishment. The affair was an astounding success. Never probably in the history of horse-whipping had punishment been so admirably and skilfully administered. Standish's clerks lined the windows and had the time of their lives. They dared not cheer; but it was obvious on which side were their sympathies.

"Funny sensation whipping a man," remarked Dare, meditatively when he told the story, "It's so devilish difficult to hit him and avoid your own legs, even when you've had a Walters to practise on."

The next day Dare received a note from Mrs. Standish, which made it clear that so far from appreciating his chivalry, she was engaged in mourning over her stricken lord, moistening his poultices with her tears.

"Queer things, women," said Dare; "chivalry is as dead as Queen Anne."

Later in the day Dare was served with a summons for assault and battery. The affair was assuming an aspect which caused him considerable anxiety. If the matter were aired in the police-court, then the whole story would come out, Millie Standish would be humiliated and Standish himself would be made utterly ridiculous. Dare decided to consult old John Brissett, his solicitor, who immediately got into touch with Standish's solicitor and told him that if the matter went into court he should supoena Fay. The result was that the lion became as a lamb. Brissett made it quite clear to Standish's solicitor, who in turn made it clear to Standish, that his respectable intentions would be entirely misunderstood. The upshot of it was that the summons was withdrawn.

"And was that the end?" I queried of Dare.

"The end?" he cried. "Good God, no! Three days later Millie Standish cut me dead at the Latimer's reception. Women are oblivious to chivalry as I said before."

"So all was well," I said.

"All was not well, my dear fellow," was Dare's reply, as he gazed up at the ceiling. "All was peculiarly and damnably ill. Horsewhipping is a luxury far beyond my means," and he started blowing rings.

"But the summons— — "

"Was withdrawn, true; but Fay was still alive alas! and with every 'tonic' she dispensed in the saloon-bar of 'The Belted Earl' she told of the noble way in which I had whipped Standish for her sake. That was Millie's doing. I could swear to it, she made Standish tell Fay that I did it because I was jealous of him and— oh, it was hell and chaos and forty publishers all rolled into one."

"But Fay?" I queried. "What of her?"

"She sent me perfumed notes (such vile perfume too) by the potman or chucker-out every other hour. Notes of adoration and of gratitude, in which the terms 'hero,' 'noble,' 'chivalrous,' with two v's, occurred at sickening intervals. I had to leave London for nearly a month, and it was at a time when I was busily engaged in a dispute with my publisher which necessitated my presence in town.

"Alas!" he concluded. "The tragedy of life is that it is always the wrong woman who appreciates a man's nobility."

"I never got no woman to appreciate my nobility wrong OR right, sir," said Bindle, at the conclusion of the story.

"Well, you're a lucky man, J.B.," said Dare. "An old fogey who lived some three thousand years ago said one of the disadvantages of matrimony was that your wife insisted on taking her meals with you."

"Did 'e really, sir?" said Bindle, greatly interested. "'I should a' like to 'ave known 'im."

"Mr. Bindle," said Sallie, "I am afraid you are a misogynist."

"I 'ope not, miss," said Bindle anxiously.

"Well you must remember that every time you say things against women you are saying something against me, because I am a woman."

"Lord, miss, don't say that," said Bindle half rising from his chair. "I never thinks o' you as a woman. You seem to be a sort of— — " and he paused.

"A sort of what?" enquired Sallie.

"Well, miss, I don't 'ardly like to say."

"Come on, speak up, J.B.," said Dick Little, "don't be a coward. We'll see that Miss Carruthers doesn't hurt you."

"You must finish your sentence, I insist," said Sallie.

"Well, miss, I was goin' to say you always seems more like a mate than a woman."

That is one of the few occasions I have seen Sallie blush. Dick Little's attentions, my devotion, Angell Herald's elaborate manners, the General's gallantry; none of them had succeeded in bringing to Sallie's face the look of pleasure that Bindle's simple remark produced.

"Thank you, Mr. Bindle, very much indeed," she said.

"But why?" asked Windover reverting to the horsewhipping affair, "why should Mrs. Standish— — "

"I expected," said Dare, "that some ass— — "

"Psychologist," suggested Windover.

"The same thing, old man," was the retort. "I expected that some psychological ass would ask why Millie Standish should behave so oddly. I will tell you. It transpired later that she had evolved a cure of her own.

"She had after all invited Fay to her flat one evening, where she met the smartest women and the cleverest men that Millie could collect. I was not included," he added.

"Fay had turned up in a pale blue satin blouse, a black skirt and white boots. She had hung herself with every ounce of metal she possessed and jingled like a cavalry charger. All the women were very nice to her, tried to draw her out; but the men just stared, first at her and then at each other. It was Millie's hour, and when Standish had put Fay into a taxi, he had wept his repentance, been taken back to Millie's heart, and all was at peace."

"So your whipping came as an anti-climax," said Windover.

"Exactly," was Dare's response.

"Alas!" remarked Windover, "A man can but do his best and a woman her worst."

CHAPTER XIV
GINGER VISITS THE NIGHT CLUB

Bindle had on more than one occasion been urged to bring Ginger to the Night Club; but Ginger finds himself "not 'oldin' wiv" so many things in life, that he is very difficult to approach. One evening, however, Bindle entered with the khaki-clad Ginger. Awkward and self-conscious, Ginger strove to disguise his nervousness under the mantle of his habitual gloom.

"We been walkin' in the Park," Bindle announced. "I been quite worried about poor old Ging. Sunday evenin' in the Park ain't no place for a young chap like 'im. It puts wrong ideas into 'is 'ead."

Ginger grumbled something in his throat and with one hand took the cigar Dick Little offered whilst with the other he grasped the glass of beer that Windover had poured out for him.

"Funny place Hyde Park on a Sunday evenin'," Bindle remarked conversationally to Sallie; "but it's a rare responsibility with a chap like Ginger."

"Now Mr. Bindle," she smiled, "if you tease him I shall be cross."

"Me tease, miss, you must be mixin' me up wi' Mr. 'Erald."

"Get along with, the yarn, J.B., tell us about the Park," urged Carruthers, who liked nothing better than to get Bindle going.

"You should 'ear wot them Australian boys says about the Daylight Bill," he continued after a pause.

"The Daylight Bill?" queried Angell Herald.

"Well, you see, sir, its like this. Them poor chaps says that they gets a gal, and then, as soon as it gets dark, it's time for 'er to go 'ome."

"But why— — ?" began Angell Herald.

"Oh, you work it out by the square root of the primitive instinct," said Dick Little, which left Angell Herald exactly where he was before.

"They're an 'ot lot, them Australians," Bindle proceeded. "Ginger says they go off with all the gals, an' 'e don't get a chance. Aint that so, ole sport?" he demanded turning to Ginger.

"I don't 'old wiv women," grumbled Ginger.

"Anyway the Kangaroos don't give yer much chance of 'oldin' 'em. Fine chaps they looks too. I don't blame the gals," Bindle added.

"Funny things gals," continued Bindle, "they'd chuck a angel for an Australian. 'Earty's got a gal to 'elp in the shop. She's a pretty bit too, yer can always trust 'Earty in little things like that. Well, she's nuts on Australians. Poor Martha gets quite worried about it. Martha's

'Earty's missis," he explained, "A rare lot o' trouble she's 'ad with Jenny. First of all the gal took up wi' the milkman, wots got an 'eart and can't get into khaki. Then she chucks 'im an' starts with Australians; an' 'e was a fivepenny milkman too, an' now 'e can't go near the 'Earty's 'ouse without it 'urtin' 'im, so poor ole Martha is a penny down on 'er milk."

Bindle paused and proceeded to pull at his pipe meditatively.

"Get ahead, man," cried Dare impatiently. "What happened to the fickle Jenny?"

"Well," continued Bindle, "she seemed to get a new Australian every night out, an' poor ole Milkcans is lookin' round for another bit o' skirt."

"Know this thou lov'st amiss and to love true,

Thou must begin again and love anew,"

quoted Dare.

"One day Martha asks Jenny why she's always out with Australians instead of our chaps. She looks down, shuffles 'er feet, nibbles the corner of 'er apron. At last she says, 'Oh, mum, it's the way they 'olds yer.'

"Yes," continued Bindle, "they're fine chaps them Australians, an' they can fight too." After a pause he continued: "Ole Spotty can't stand 'em, though. Spotty's got somethink wrong with 'is lungs and the doctor says to 'im, 'Spotty ole card, it's outdoors or underground. The choice is with you.'

"So instead o' becomin' a member o' parliament, Spotty goes round takin' pennies for lettin' people sit down on the chairs in the Park. It means fourpence 'alfpenny an 'our now an' rheumatism later.

"Them Australians can't understand bein' asked a penny to sit down, and sometimes they refuses to pay, thinking it's a do. It's a shame not to let 'em sit down for nothink, after they come all them miles to fight. So Spotty soon learns to sort of overlook 'em.

"One day an inspector reports 'im to the guv'nor, an' 'e was 'auled up an' asked to tell all about it. 'E did, also 'ow one of 'em offered to fight 'im for the penny. Spotty's a slip of a thing like a war sausage.

"'I took up this 'ere job,' says Spotty, 'to get well, not as a short cut to the 'orspital,' and he offered to resign; but they're short o' men an' Spotty is still takin' pennies, when 'e can get 'em without scrappin'.

"Lord, the things Spotty's told me about Hyde Park. It ain't no place for me. I told Mrs. B. one night, leastwise I told 'er some, an' she says, 'The King ought to stop it.'" Bindle grinned. "I can see 'im goin' round a-stoppin' it by 'avin' all the chairs put two yards apart, an' bein' late for 'is supper."

"Are you a royalist, J.B.?" enquired Windover languidly.

"A wot, sir?" enquired Bindle.

"Do you believe in kings?"

"I believe in our King." There was decision in Bindle's voice. "'E's a sport, same as 'is father was. I'm sick of all this talk about a republic." Disgust was clearly expressed upon Bindle's face and in his voice. "Down at the yard they're always jawin' about the revolution wot's comin'."

"I don't 'old wiv kings," broke in Ginger. "There's goin' to be a revolution."

"'Ullo Ging, you woke up? Well ole son, wot's wrong wi' George Five?"

"Look wot 'e corsts, an' you an' me 'as to pay, an' everything goin' up like 'ell."

"'Ush, Ginger, 'ush, there's a lady 'ere."

Ginger looked awkwardly at Sallie, who smiled her reassurance.

"'I s'pose, Ginger, yer thinks you're goin' to get a republic with a pound o' tea," said Bindle good-humouredly.

"There's goin' to be a revolution," persisted Ginger doggedly. Ginger logic is repetition. "After the war," he added.

"An' wot jer goin' to revolute about?" enquired Bindle, gazing at Ginger's face, which Windover has described as "freckled with stupidity."

For a few minutes Ginger was silent, thinking laboriously.

"Look at the price of beer?" he at length challenged with inspiration.

"Well, Ging, ain't you an ole 'uggins. 'Jer think you'll get cheap beer if yer makes George and Mary 'op it? Not you, ole son. Wot you'll most likely get is no beer at all, same as in America."

"That's a lie!" We were all startled at the anger in Ginger's voice, as he flashed a sullen challenge round the room.

"Don't get 'uffy, ole sport. Wot's a lie?" enquired Bindle, unmoved by Ginger's outburst.

"That they ain't got no beer in America," snarled Ginger.

"J.B. is quite right," murmured Windover soothingly. "In some States there's no drink of any sort."

Ginger gazed from one to the other, bewilderment and alarm stamped upon his face.

"Well I'm— — " began Ginger.

"Surprised," broke in Bindle. "O' course you are. Fancy bein' in the army without anythink to wash it down.

"Now, Ginger," said Bindle after a pause, "tell the General 'ow 'appy you are bein' a soldier."

"I don't 'old wiv the army," was Ginger's gloomy response.

"What!" There was the light of battle in the General's eye. "Then why the devil did you enlist?" he demanded in his most aggressive parade manner.

"To get away," was Ginger's enigmatical response.

"To get away! To get away from what?" demanded the General.

"You see, sir," explained Bindle, "Ginger ain't 'appy in 'is 'ome life. 'E's got a wife an' three kids and— — "

"Jawin' an' squallin'," interrupted Ginger vindictively.

"Why don't you like the army?" demanded the General.

"Don't 'old wiv orficers."

"With officers! Why?"

"Order yer about."

"How the devil would you know what to do if they didn't order you about?" demanded the General rapidly losing his temper.

"Don't 'old wiv the army," was the grumbled retort.

It is Ginger's method, when faced with an awkward question, to fall back upon his inner defences by announcing that he "don't 'old wiv" whatever it is under discussion.

"If you don't hold with the army, with officers, with wives and children, then what do you hold with?" demanded the General angrily.

"Beer," was the laconic response, uttered without the vestige of a smile.

Ginger personifies gloom. He would if he could snatch the sun's ray from a dewdrop, or the joyousness from a child's laugh. It is constitutional.

"Poor ole Ginger's 'appier when 'e's miserable," Bindle explained; "but 'e's a rare good sort at 'eart is Ging. 'E once bought a cock canary, wot the man told 'im would sing like a prize bird; but when the yaller comes orf an' there warn't no song, and the bird started a-layin' eggs, it sort o' broke poor ole Ging. up. 'E ain't never been the same man since, 'ave yer, ole sport?"

Ginger muttered something inaudible, the tone of which suggested blood.

"If you could catch that cove you'd be 'oldin' 'im, eh Ging?"

"Blast 'im!" exploded Ginger.

Shortly afterwards Ginger took an ungracious leave. The Night Club saw him no more.

On the Sunday following Bindle arrived early, hilarious with excitement.

"'Old me, 'Orace," he cried joyously, and two of "Tims'" men supported him in the approved manner of the prize-ring, flapping handkerchiefs before his face. Presently Bindle reassumed control of his limbs.

"What's the joke?" enquired Dick Little.

"Joke!" cried Bindle. "Joke! 'E re 'old me again."

After further ministrations he explained. On the previous day he had met one of Ginger's mates, who had told him that Ginger was undergoing seven days C.B. for fighting in the guardroom.

"An' wot jer think 'e was fighting about?" enquired Bindle, his face crinkled with smiles.

We gave it up.

"Because one of 'is mates says we're goin' to 'ave a republic! The poor chap's in 'orspital now," he added, "a-learnin' to believe in kings, and poor ole Ginger's learnin' that it ain't wise to believe too much in anythink."

"Well, here's to Private Ginger, loyalist," cried Jim Colman, and we drank the toast in a way that brought the General hurrying up from below.

"I seem to been 'avin' quite a lot o' things 'appen last week," remarked Bindle as he unscrewed the stopper of a beer-bottle on the sideboard, and poured the contents into the pewter tankard that Sallie had given him. After a long and refreshing drink he continued tantalisingly—

"Funny 'ow things 'appen to me. Cheer-o! Archie," this to Old Archie who had just entered, his face looking more than ever like a withered apple in which were set a pair of shrewd, but kindly eyes.

"Tellin' the tale, Joe," he remarked. Then turning to the rest of us he added, "Suppose poor old Joe was to forget 'ow to talk. Evenin', m'lord," this with an upward movement of his hand as Windover entered.

"There ain't no fear o' that, Archie my lad," replied Bindle. "I'm as likely to forget 'ow to talk as you are to remember to put the cawfee into the stuff yer sells for more'n it's worth."

"What's been happening?" demanded Blint.

"I see Mr. Angell 'E rald the other day," Bindle remarked. "I was on the tail-board o' the van with ole Wilkes, 'im wot coughs to keep 'im from swallowing flies."

"Did he see you?" enquired Dick Little.

"If 'e didn't see me, there wasn't no excuse for 'im not 'earin' Wilkie's cough. They wouldn't 'ave 'im as a special constable. Rude to 'im they was. Poor ole Wilkie ain't forgot it, 'e's a bit sensitive like, not bein' married."

"Never mind about Wilkes," broke in Tom Little. "Get oh with the story, J.B."

At times Bindle has a tendency to wander into by-paths of reminiscence.

"It was in the Strand," he continued, "an' to make sure of Mr. Angell 'Erald not bein' disappointed I cheero'd 'im. 'E sort o' looked round frightened-like, then 'e disappeared into a teashop like a rabbit in an 'ole. S'pose 'e suddenly remembered 'e was tea-thirsty," and Bindle looked round solemnly.

"Perhaps he didn't hear you," ventured Dick Little.

"When I cheero a cove, an' Wilkie coughs at 'im, well if 'e don't 'ear then 'e ought to be seen to, because it's serious. Why the cop on point mentioned it to me. Said we'd set the motor-busses shyin' if we didn't stop. 'E was quite 'urt about it. Seemed upset-like about poor ole Wilkie's cough. No: 'e 'eard us right enough."

"He may not have recognised you," the Boy ventured, knowing full well that Angell Herald would not be seen exchanging salutations with a man on the tail-board of a pantechnicon.

But Bindle merely closed his left eye and placed the forefinger of his right hand at the side of his nose.

At that moment Angell Herald entered the room. He glanced, a little anxiously I thought, at Bindle who, however, greeted him with unaffected good-humour.

"When you come in, sir," he explained cheerily, "I was jest tellin' 'ow me an' Wilkie ran across 'is Lordship last week. Me an' Wilkie was on the tail-board o' the van; but 'is Lordship come up an'— wot jer think?"

Bindle gazed round the room triumphantly. Angell Herald looked extremely unhappy. Windover, on the contrary, seemed unusually interested. Having centred upon himself the attention of the whole room Bindle proceeded,

"'E took us into a swell place an' stood us a dinner. Lord, 'ow they did look to see us, me an' Wilkie in our aprons, 'is Lordship in 'is red tabs an' a gold rim to 'is cap, an' a red band round it."

Bindle was enjoying himself hugely, especially as he saw that Angell Herald was becoming more and more uncomfortable.

"We 'ad champagne an' oysters, an' soup an'— — Well I thought Wilkie 'ud never stop." He broke off to light his pipe, when it was in full blast he continued.

"Presently a cove in an 'igh collar comes up an' says polite like to 'is lordship—

"'Would you kindly ask that gentleman to 'urry with 'is soup, sir,' meanin' Wilkie, 'there's a gentleman over there wot says 'e can't 'ear the band, an' this is 'is favourite tune.'"

"Mr. Bindle!" cried Sallie, who is very sensitive upon the subject of table manners.

"I'm sorry, miss, but you see poor ole Wilkie never 'ad no mother to teach 'im. Yes," he continued, "we 'ad a rare ole time, me an' Wilkie."

Angell Herald looked from Bindle to Windover. His veneer of self-complacency had been badly punctured.

"By the way, J.B.," said Windover, "I want you to come to lunch with me again on Saturday. You'll come, Little and you, Boy."

It was Bindle's turn to look surprised. That is how he got a real "dinner" with a lord, and Angell Herald had a lesson by which he probably failed to profit. To this day he believes Bindle's story of the mythical lunch. Bindle has never forgiven Angell Herald his "men's stories," and he unites with the Boy in scoring off him whenever possible. Sometimes Dick Little and I have to take a strong line with both delinquents. Fortunately Angell Herald is more often than not oblivious of what is taking place.

Sometimes we have a night devoted to Bindle's views on life. His philosophy is a thing devoid of broideries and frills. It is the essence of his own experience. Once when Dare had been talking upon the subject of ideals, Bindle had remarked:

"Very pretty to talk about, but they ain't much use in the furniture-movin' line. One in the eye is more likely to make a man be'ave than a month's jawin' about wot 'Earty calls 'brotherly love.'"

Bindle's good-nature makes it possible for him to say without offence what another man could not even hint at.

Windover once remarked that Bindle would go through life saying and doing things impossible to any but a prize-fighter.

"An' why a bruiser, sir?" Bindle had enquired.

"Well, few men care to punch the head of a professional boxer," was the retort.

"It ain't wot yer say, sir," Bindle had remarked, obviously pleased at the compliment. "It's wot's be'ind the words. I ain't got time to look for angels in trousers, or saints in skirts. There ain't many of us wot ain't got a tear or an 'ole somewhere, but it ain't 'elpin' things to put it in the papers."

"But," Jim Dare, one of "Tims'" men, broke in wickedly, "without criticism there'd be no progress."

Bindle was on him like a flash.

"If an angel's lost 'is tail feathers," he retorted, "you bet the other angels ain't goin' to make a song about it. If they was the right sort of angels they'd pull their own out, to show that tail-feathers ain't everythink."

We made many attempts to get at Bindle's views upon the Hereafter: but although by nature as open as the day, there are some things about which he is extremely reticent. One evening in answer to a direct challenge he replied,

"Well, I don't rightly know, I ain't been taught things; but I got a sort of idea that Gawd's a sight better man than Joe Bindle, an' that's why I can't stick 'Earty's Gawd. 'E ain't Gawd no more'n I'm the Kayser." Then after a pause he had added, "If Gawd's goin' to be Gawd 'E's got to be a mystery. Why there's some coves wot seem to know more about wot Gawd's goin' to do than wot they've 'ad for dinner."

Dick Little never lost an opportunity of getting Bindle started upon his favourite subject— marriage. One night he announced that his brother Tom had become engaged to be married.

"'E's wot?" interrogated Bindle.

"He's done it, J.B.," Dick Little had replied with a laugh.

Bindle said nothing; but we awaited Tom Little's arrival with no little eagerness. When he entered, Bindle fixed him with a remorseless eye.

"Wot's this I 'ear, sir?" he enquired.

"What's what?" Tom Little enquired, becoming very pink, and casting a furious glance in his brother's direction.

Tom Little's demeanour left no doubt as to his guilt. For some moments Bindle regarded him gravely. Tom Little proceeded to light a cigarette; but he was obviously ill at ease.

"Wot's the use o' me tellin' yer all about women," Bindle demanded, "when, as soon as my back's turned yer goes an' does it. Silly sort of thing to do, I call it."

"Don't be an ass, J.B." Tom Little strove to carry off the affair lightly; but Bindle was Rhadamanthine.

"I told yer not to," he continued, then after a pause, "Course she's got pretty 'air an' eyes, an' made yer feel funny an' all that; but you jest wait. Mrs. B. 'ad all them things, an' look at 'er now. She's about as soft-'earted as a cop is to a cove wot's 'carryin' the banner.'" *

* Walking the streets through the night

"Shut up, J.B.," said Tom Little, looking round as if seeking some loophole of escape.

"Well, sir," said Bindle with an air of resignation, "it's your funeral, but I'm sorry, I 'ope Gawd'll 'elp yer; but I know 'e won't."

Another evening Bindle had opened the proceedings by his customary "Miss an' gentlemen, I got a warnin' to give yer. There's only two things wot a cove 'as got to fight against, one is a wife in 'is bosom, an' the other is various veins in 'is legs. An' now I'll call for the story."

CHAPTER XV
A DRAMATIC ENGAGEMENT

The Night Club has neither rules nor officials; that is what makes it unique. Bindle, Dick Little and I form a sort of unofficial committee of management. No one questions our rulings, because our rulings are so infrequent as scarcely to be noticeable. One of our great trials, almost our only trial, is the suppression of Angell Herald. He is for ever proposing to introduce intimates of his own, and we are often hard put to it to find excuses for his not being allowed to do so.

One evening he scored heavily against the "committee," by bringing with him a tall man with long hair, a blue chin and an eye that spoke of a thirst with long arrears to be worked off.

His first remark was "Good evening, gentlemen," as if he were entering the commercial room of a hotel. Windover screwed his glass firmly into his left eye. Windover's monocle is always a social barometer— it "places" a man irrevocably. His face never shows the least expression; but it is quite possible to see from his bearing whether or no a new arrival be possible.

"Allow me to introduce my friend, Mr. Leonard Gimp, the actor," said Angell Herald.

"Haaa! Very pleased to meet you, gentlemen, very pleased indeed, Haaa!" came somewhere from Mr. Gimp's middle, via his mouth.

As host Dick Little came forward and shook hands: but it was clear from the look in his eye that he shared our homicidal views with regard to Angell Herald.

"Haaa! and how are you, Mr. Little?" enquired Gimp genially.

Little muttered something inaudible to the rest of us.

"That's right!" said Gimp in hearty but hollow tones. "What wonderful weather we're having," he continued beaming upon the rest of us, as if determined to put us at our ease.

"Wonderful weather," he repeated.

He was a strange creature, with ill-fitting garments and soiled linen. Before he began to speak he said "Haaa!" When he had finished speaking he said "Haaa!" If he had nothing at all to say, which was seldom, he said "Haaa!" His air was confidential and his manner friendly. It was obvious that he strove to model himself on the late Sir Henry Irving. The world held for him only one thing— the Drama; and the Drama only one interpreter— himself.

Gimp sat down and, stretching out his legs, bent over and stroked them from instep to loins, beaming upon us the while.

"May I offer you a cigarette?" he queried, picking up a box from the mantelpiece and proffering to Dick Little one of his own cigarettes.

Gimp seemed to be under the impression that he had come to entertain us and he began to talk. His sentences invariably began with "Haaa! I remember in 1885," or some other date, and we quickly learned that with him dates were a danger signal.

His idea of conversation was a monologue. As we sat listening, we wondered how we should ever stop the flow of eloquence. He plunged into a memory involving a quotation from a drama in which, as far as we could gather, he had made one of the greatest hits the theatrical world had ever witnessed. His enthusiasm brought him to his feet. We sat and smoked and listened, mutely conscious that the situation was beyond us.

Angell Herald was the only man present, besides Gimp himself, who seemed to be satisfied. The rest of us felt that there was only one hope, and that lay in Bindle, who was unaccountably late. Bindle, we felt sure, would be able to rise to the occasion, and he did.

Gimp had reached a most impassioned scene in which the heroine denounces the villain, who is a coiner. Bindle entered the room unobserved by Gimp. For a few moments he stood watching the scene with intense interest. Gimp had reached the climax of the scene in which the heroine says to the villain, "Go! Your heart is as base as the coins you make." He paused, pointing dramatically in the direction of Windover.

"'Ullo! 'Amlet," said Bindle genially from behind.

Gimp span round as if he had been shot, and gazed down at Bindle in indignant surprise.

"Cheero! Where'd you spring from?" continued Bindle.

"Sir?" said Gimp.

"Your wrong," said Bindle, "it's plain Joe Bindle, Sir Joseph later perhaps; but not yet."

Bindle smiled up innocently at Gimp, who gazed round him as if seeking for some explanation of Bindle's presence, then a weak and weary smile fluttered across his features, and he walked over to the side-board and mixed himself a whisky and soda.

We seized the opportunity to break off Gimp's demonstrations of his histrionic powers. We gave him a cigar, and every time he started "Haaa! I remember in 18— — " somebody butted in and cut him short.

That evening Bindle was in a wicked mood. He flagrantly encouraged Gimp to talk "shop," "feeding the furnace of his self-conceit," as Dare whispered across me to Sallie.

"I went to the theatre last week," said Bindle with guile, "but I didn't see you there, sir."

"Haaa! no!" said Gimp, "I'm restin'."

"Sort o' worn out," said Bindle sympathetically.

Gimp looked sharply at Bindle, who gazed back with disarming innocence. "Haaa! a nervous breakdown," he replied.

"To judge by his nose, neuritis of the elbow," said Carruthers sotto voce.

"What was the piece you saw, J.B.?" enquired Roger Blint.

"FRISKY FLORRIE. Them plays didn't ought to be allowed. Made me 'ot all over, it did." Then turning to Gimp he added, "I'm surprised at you, sir, sayin' there ain't nothink like the drama."

"That is not the Deraaama," cried Gimp. "That's a pollution," his filmy eyes rolled and he jerked his head backwards in what was apparently the dramatic conception of indignation.

"Fancy that, an' me not knowin' it," was Bindle's comment.

"Haaa!" said Gimp.

"Won't you say one o' your pieces for us, sir?" enquired Bindle. "I'd like to 'ear real drama."

Gimp looked blankly at Bindle.

"J.B. means won't you recite," explained Dare in even tones.

Gimp was on his feet instantly, vowing that he was delighted. For a moment he was plunged in deep thought, his chin cupped in his left hand, the elbow supported by the palm of his right hand. It was extremely effective. Suddenly he gave utterance to the inevitable "Haaa!" and we knew that the gods had breathed inspiration upon him.

Straightening himself, he shot his hands still further through his already short coat sleeves, and gazed round. Raising his left hand he cried—

"Haaa! Shakespeare."

Then he broke out into

"Ferends, Rhomans, Cohuntrymen lehend me your eeeeeears."

Quintilian was thrown overboard: for there was nothing restrained in Leonard Gimp's declamation. His arms waved like flails, his legs, slack at the knee, took strides and then "as you were'd" with bewildering rapidity. It was ju-jitsu, foils and Swedish drill all mixed up together. One moment he was exhorting Windover, the next he was telling Sallie in a voice that throbbed like the engaged signal on the telephone how "gerievously hath Cæsar paid for it." The emotion engendered by the munificence of Cæsar's will produced a new action, which broke an electric globe and, midst the shattering of glass, the doom of Brutus was sealed.

"That is Shakespeare's Deraaama," he declared, as he resumed his seat and proceeded once more to stroke his legs.

It was clear to all of us that something had to be done, and it was Dick Little who did it.

Jocelyn Dare is a magnificent elocutionist, although he can seldom be prevailed upon to recite. To-night, however, he readily responded to Dick Little's invitation. He selected Henry V's exhortation to the troops before Harfleur. After Gimp's vigorous demonstration, Dare's almost immobile delivery seemed like calm after a storm. He looked a picturesque figure as he stood, from time to time tossing back the flood of black hair that cascaded down his forehead. He has a beautiful voice, deep, resonant, flexible and under perfect control.

Bindle seemed hypnotised. His pipe forgotten he leaned forward eagerly as if fearful of losing a word. Gimp sat with a puzzled look upon his face, impressed in spite of himself.

It was the first time the Night Club had heard Dare, and when he concluded there was a lengthy silence, broken at last by Gimp, whose voice sounded like an anæmic drum after Dare's magnificent tones.

"Haaa! thank you, sir, excellent," he cried patronisingly. "You should go on the stage, haaa!"

"Well that knocks the bottom out of ole Shakespeare any'ow," said Bindle with decision, as he proceeded to light his neglected pipe.

"It is Shakespeare," said Sallie.

Bindle looked at her over the lighted match, then to Dare and on to Gimp. Finally he completed the operation of lighting his pipe.

"Well," he said somewhat enigmatically, "that proves wot they say about there bein' somethink in the man be'ind the gun."

Soon after Gimp took his departure with Angell Herald, leaving us with the consciousness that the evening had not been a success.

"You took it out of ole 'Amlet, sir," said Bindle with keen enjoyment. "That ole phonograph in 'is middle sounds sort o' funny arter 'earin' you. An' didn't 'e throw 'isself about, broke your globe too, sir," this to Dick Little, "an' then never said 'e was sorry."

"He regarded it as the jetsam of art," said Windover.

"P'raps you're right, sir," was Bindle's comment.

That evening resulted in the committee making it generally understood that no one was to be introduced to the Night Club without his name first being submitted to and approved by Bindle, Dick Little and myself.

Some weeks later I happened by chance to run across Gimp in the West End. He thrust himself upon me and clung like a limpet, insisting that I should have what he called "a tonic," which in his case consisted of a continuous stream of glasses of port wine. When we parted some two hours later I had a story, in return for which he had received ten glasses of port wine, for which I paid, and five shillings. The last named he had obtained by a "Dear old boy, lend me a dollar till next Tuesday morning.

"Good-bye, my dear boy, God bless you," he cried with emotion as he pocketed the two half-crowns and left me, turning when he had taken some half-a-dozen steps to cry once more, "God bless you."

He did not inquire my address, and I am sure he did not know my name, so that in all probability he is to this day walking London searching for me to repay that dollar.

The story, however, was worth, not only the dollar but the port wine.

"Fancy Old 'Amlet 'avin' a story like that in 'is tummy," was Bindle's comment.

This was Leonard Gimp's story:

I

"But how do you know I can't do it, Mr. Telford, if you won't let me try?" There was something suspiciously like a sob in Elsie Gwyn's voice as she leaned forward across Roger Telford's table. "Please let me try, it means so much to me."

"My dear girl, a part like that requires experience and a knowledge that you could not possibly possess. The whole play turns on that one character. Now don't be disappointed," he continued kindly, "you're doing very well and your time will come. Now you must run away like a good girl, because I've scores of things to do. I shan't forget you and I'll cast you for something later.

Seeing that further argument was useless the girl rose to go.

"Good-bye, Mr. Telford," she said soberly, blinking her eyes more than seemed necessary, "I'm sure you don't mean to be unkind; but really you ought to give me a chance before judging me. It's not quite sporting of you."

Telford placed his hand for a moment on her shoulder. "Now cheer up, little girl," he said, "Your time will come." He opened the door and closed it again after her— Telford's courtesy and kindness were the "joke" of the profession.

Roger Telford returned to the table and for a few minutes sat pondering deeply. He was the most successful theatrical manager in London. Everything he turned his hand to seemed to prosper. Rival managers said he had the devil's own luck; but instinctively they knew that it was the sureness of his judgment that resulted in one success after another being associated with his name.

In the profession he was regarded a "white man." Many laughed at him for being a prude, and he was known among the inner circle as "Mrs. Telford," on account of his attitude towards the girls in his companies. He had been known to knock a man down to teach him how to behave to a "Telford girl." Those who could not get into his companies sneered at him as "a fish in an ice box"; but those who were in his employ knew what a good friend he could be. He was a bachelor and possessed a reputation that not even his worst enemy could sully. Men affected to despise him, and a certain class of theatrical girl looked upon him with contempt; but Roger Telford's was a great name in the theatrical world.

"Little Elsie Gwyn wanted the part of Jenny Burrow in THE SIXTH SENSE," he remarked a few minutes later to Tom Bray, his stage manager at the Lyndhurst Theatre.

Bray shook his head. He was a man of few words.

"Exactly what I told her," said Telford; "but where the devil are we going to get anyone? There's Esther Grant, Phyllis Cowan, Lallie Moore; but none of them have got it in 'em. They're just low comedy turns. This thing wants something more than that. It wants dramatic grip, it wants guts, and I'm hanged if I know of a woman who's got 'em."

"There's not much time," was the comment of the stage manager.

"Of all the damned uninspiring chaps, you beat the lot, Tom," laughed Telford. "Here's the infernal show getting into rehearsal on Monday, and you're as calm as an oyster."

"Better cast the understudy, let her do it for a time," said Bray.

"It looks as if we shall have to fall back on Helen Strange," grumbled Telford.

"She'll wreck the show, sure," commented the stage manager.

"Damn!" said Telford, as he crushed his hat on his head, seized his stick and gloves and went out to lunch.

II

Elsie Gwyn had been on the stage three years, two of which had been spent in the provinces, principally in understudying. Like many other ambitious people, she told herself that she had never had a chance.

"It's rotten," she confided to a friend. "They always cast you according to your face. They're as bad as the American managers, who are always talking about 'the type.' Just because I've got fair hair and small features and blue eyes, and a sort of washed out appearance (as a matter of fact Elsie Gwyn was exquisitely pretty with golden hair, refined features and deep blue eyes, almost violet in tint), they cast me for vicars' daughters, milk-and-water misses and the like. I am sure I've got drama in me, only no one will give me the chance to get it out."

"Oh! dry up, Elsie," her friend had responded, "you want to be Juliet in your first year."

Elsie Gwyn had walked down the stairs to the stage-door of the Lyndhurst Theatre feeling that if anyone spoke crossly to her she would inevitably cry.

"It isn't fair," she muttered to herself after saying good morning to the stage doorkeeper, "it isn't fair to say I can't do it without giving me a chance. It's rotten of them, absolutely rotten."

She seemed to find some comfort from this expression of opinion.

"When I'm famous, and I shall be famous some day," she told herself, "he'll be sorry that he didn't give me my chance." With this comforting assurance Elsie Gwyn entered the small Soho restaurant she frequented when in the West End and ordered lunch.

III

THE SIXTH SENSE had been put into rehearsal, and still the part of Jenny Burrow had not been cast. Bray had urged upon Telford the necessity of securing Helen Strange; but Telford had hung out.

"I believe in my luck, old man," he said, "something will turn up. I shall wait till the end of the week."

This was Thursday. Telford and his stage-manager were in the throes of producing THE SIXTH SENSE from a company that, according to Tom Bray, hadn't a single sense, among the lot. The theatre was all gloom and strange shadows. The company was grouped round the stage, leaving a clear space in the centre for those actually rehearsing. Some sat on the two or three chairs available and three odd boxes, the rest stood about conversing in undertones.

To the uninitiated it would have seemed impossible that a play could be produced out of such chaos. It was difficult to disentangle the dramatist's lines from Telford's comments and instructions. He was probably the most hard-working producer in London, and the most difficult: but his company knew that by working with him whole-heartedly they were striving for a common object— success. There was less grumbling at his theatres than at any other in the kingdom. If he blamed unstintingly he paid well, and to have been with Telford was in itself a testimonial.

"Good God!" he broke out, "you make love as if the woman were a gas-pipe."

The youth addressed flushed and turning to Telford rapped back, "Let me choose my own woman and I'll show you how to make love, Mr. Telford."

Telford walked over to him and putting his hand on his shoulder said, "My boy, I like that. Go ahead, do it your own way and you'll get there."

That was Roger Telford all over. He understood human nature. He knew that a man who could rap back an answer such as he had just received had imagination, and he was there merely to direct that imagination.

"That's better," he cried as the youth was warming to his work. "Hi! steady though, not too much realism in rehearsals, keep that for the first night."

"My God!" cried Telford a few minutes later as he thrust his fingers through his hair. "That's not Jenny Burrow, that's THE PILGRIM'S PROGRESS. The understudy was not a success."

Hour dragged after weary hour, lunch time came, three quarters of an hour, and then back again. There seemed no continuity. First a bit of this act then a bit of that: it was like building up a cinema film. It was depressing work this preparing for the public amusement. It would have been more depressing; but for the vitality and personal magnetism of Telford!

Two o'clock dragged on to three, three to half-past three, and thoughts were turning towards tea-time, the half hour that was permitted at four o'clock, when a startling interruption occurred. From the direction of the stage-door a woman's voice was heard raised in anger.

"Engaged is he," it cried. "Too busy to see me? I DON'T think. You just run along and tell him that Florrie's here and wants to see him, and if he don't see her she'll raise hell." The murmur of the stage doorkeeper's voice was heard.

"Here, get out of the way," said the voice. A moment after a girl bounced on to the stage. She was young, stylishly dressed, fair as far as could be seen through her thick veil. The stage doorkeeper followed close upon her heels muttering protests. Turning on him like a fury the girl shouted:

"Here, clear out of it if you don't want a thick ear."

The man hurriedly stepped back a few paces. The girl who had announced herself as Florrie gave a swift look round, then spotting Telford went directly up to him.

"Said you were too busy, Roj. Not too to see Florrie, old sport, what?"

Telford gazed at the girl in astonishment.

"You've made a mistake, I think," he said coldly.

"Oh, listen to the band," she sang. "Look here, what's your lay, what are you after?"

Telford was conscious that the eyes of the company were upon him. "I'm afraid I don't know you, and you've made a mistake."

"I never saw the lady before so she can't be mine you see," sang Florrie, who seemed to be in high spirits.

"I'm busy," said Telford, "and I must ask you to go. You've made a mistake."

"Is your name Roger Telford, or is it not?"

"I am Mr. Telford, yes."

"Oh! well, Mr. Telford, I'm Florrie. Never heard o' Florrie before, I suppose. Look here Roj., none of your swank. You ain't been keepin' me for two years to give me the bird like this. You thought you'd done me, didn't you, writing that letter and saying all was over."

"I tell you," said Telford with some asperity, "that I do not know you."

"Oh, Roger boy, Roger boy," said Florrie, wagging her finger at him. "Aint you the blooming limit?" She placed her hands upon her lips, threw her body back and regarded him with good-humoured aggressiveness.

"I tell you I've never seen you before. If you refuse to go I shall have you removed."

Telford's anger was rising.

"Oh! you're stickin' it on that lay, are you? All right, I'm your bird. Never seen me before, haven't you? I suppose you don't remember happening to meet me in "The Pocock Arms" two years ago last March do you? You don't happen to remember seeing me home. You don't happen to remember taking a flat for me. You don't happen to remember giving me money and jewels. You don't happen to remember getting tired of me? And I suppose you don't happen to remember writing a letter and saying that it was all over and that you would give me fifty pounds to be off and all the furniture. Do you happen to remember any of those things, Mister Telford?"

Telford looked round him bewildered. The expression on the faces of his company left him in no doubt as to their view of the situation.

"I— I don't know who you are or what you mean," he stuttered. "And— and if you don't leave this er— er— place I shall send for a policeman. Saunders," he called to the stage doorkeeper who was still hovering about.

"Oh you will, will you," screamed Florrie, working herself up into a passion. "You'll send for a policeman will you? Go on Saunders, if that's your ugly name, fetch a policeman. That's just what I want. We'll soon clear up this matter. You just fetch a bloomin' policeman. Fetch two policemen while you're about it, and bring a handful of specials as well." She laughed stridently at her joke. As her anger rose her aitches disappeared, her idiom became coarser.

Seeing that Saunders hesitated she cried "Well! Why don't you go?" Then she turned upon Telford. "Send 'im for a rotten policeman. Go on. You dirty tyke. You mucky-souled liar. Never met me before? Never even seen me. After what 'as 'appened and what you done for me. I was a good gurl till I met you. Why don't you send for a policeman?"

Saunders looked interrogatingly at Telford, who shook his head.

"Ah!" screamed the girl. "I thought you wouldn't send for no policeman."

"She's mad," muttered Telford under his breath. He looked helplessly about him. If there were a scene it might get into the papers, it would certainly be a nine days wonder in the "profession."

"Now look 'ere," shrilled Florrie to the assembled company, "that dirty tyke says 'e don't know me, never seen me before this very hour. What about this?" She produced a photograph from one of the large pockets in her frock. "To the only woman in the world, from Roger," she read.

She held out a recent photograph of Telford for the company to see. The writing was certainly very like his. Tom Bray came forward and examined it. He looked grave.

"Well!" cried Florrie to Bray, "Is it like 'im. I suppose you're Tom Bray, 'is stage manager. 'E's told me about you. Called you an oyster because you never get flurried, said all you wanted was a bit o' lemon."

Tom Bray started and looked swiftly at Telford. That was a favourite phrase of the chief's.

"It's a forgery," almost shouted Telford, making a clutch at the photograph.

"No you don't, ducky," was Florrie's laughing retort. "We'll put you away to bye-bye," and she tucked the photograph down her blouse.

"What is it you want with me?" asked Telford mechanically.

"Oh! that's it, is it," she cried. "You think I want money. You think I'm a blackmailer, do you? You just offer me money and I'll fling it in yer ugly face, I will, you dirty tyke. I want to know what you mean by writing me that letter— chucking me after what you done. That's what I want to know. I'm going to let all the world know what sort of a man you are, Mrs. Telford. I suppose you've found someone amongst all these gurls here what you like better'n me."

Telford looked round him as if expecting inspiration from somewhere. On his forehead stood beads of perspiration which he mopped up with his handkerchief.

Suddenly Florrie flopped down upon the stage and began to sob hysterically. "Roger boy, don't chuck me," she wailed, trying to clutch his knees, he stepped back in time to avoid her. "Don't chuck me. I always been true to you, I 'ave. You oughtn't to do the dirty on me like this. I won't worry you, only just let me see you sometimes."

The girl's self-abasement was so complete, her emotion so genuine that more than one of those present felt an uncomfortable sensation in their throats.

"What in God's name am I to do?" Telford cried, half to himself; but looking in the direction of the low comedian, Ben Walters.

"You might marry the girl," said Ben. He regretted his words the moment they were uttered.

In a flash Florrie was on her feet, her humility gone, her eyes flaming. "Who are you?" she screamed, turning on him like a fury. "You're the funny man I s'pose, but you ain't nearly so funny as what you think. Anyone could be funny with a face like yours. God made you a damn sight funnier than what you know." Then with withering scorn, "I've seen better things won in a raffle."

Never had a comedian looked less funny than Walters at that moment. With an almost imperceptible movement he edged away from his persecutor.

"Yes, that's right. You slip off, and if you can get anyone to buy your face, don't you ask too much for it. Well! What are you going to do?" This to Telford to whom she turned once more. Her movements were as swift as her emotional changes.

"I— I told you you've made a mistake," repeated Telford; but he was conscious of the futility of the remark.

"And I tell you you're a liar," replied Florrie. "A gurl ain't likely to make a mistake about a man what's done to her what you've done to me. I was a good gurl till I met you." There was a break in her voice that was perilously like a sob. "Look what you done for me, look, look. Oh! my God!" She buried her face in her handkerchief. Her whole body shaken with sobs, then slowly her knees gave way beneath her and she sank in a heap on the stage, still sobbing hysterically.

"Jenny Burrow in real life," muttered Tom Bray. "If she could only act it all."

"Oh, Roj," she cried through her handkerchief. "Oh! Roj-boy, you've broken my heart. I love you so. I'd 'ave done anything for you. I did. I— I— an' now what's to become of me? What's fifty pounds to a gurl whose heart's broken? You— you played the dirty on me, Roj-boy, you played the dirty on me. They got to know all about it at home and father won't let mother see me. I— I— we was such pals, mother an' me, an' it's all through you; but— but— " she struggled to her feet with heaving breast. "I ain't done yet. I'll pay you back, you and your play-actors. I was a decent gurl before I met you. You— you— dirty tyke." She fell back on the old phrase from sheer poverty of vocabulary.

"You're like all men," she shrieked. "Like every cursed one of 'em. You come into a gurl's life, ruin it, then off you go and you give her money; but I'll break you this time, I'll break you, I'll smash you, Roger Telford, I'll smash you. Damn you! Blast you! May hell open and swallow you."

The vindictiveness in the girl's voice made even the most hardened sinner shudder.

"I'm goin' to do myself in," she continued, "there's nothing left for me; but I'll leave behind me the whole story, I'll ruin you, just as you've ruined me. These are your friends round you, these 'ere men and women. Look at their faces, look at 'em, see what they think of you now; you stinkin', low-bred swine."

Telford looked on the point of collapse. Someone gently propelled a chair towards him, on which he sank gazing round him stupidly.

Suddenly Florrie gave a wild hysterical shriek and fell. For a moment her limbs twitched spasmodically, then she lay very still. She had fainted. Several of the girls ran forward and began fumbling about with the fastenings of her clothes. They removed her hat and veil, and one of them uttered a cry of surprise.

Suddenly Florrie sat up, and those about her, as if impelled by their instinct for the dramatic, stood aside that Telford could see her.

It was Elsie Gwyn.

"Please Mr. Telford," she said smiling, and in her natural voice, "won't you give me a trial in the part of Jenny Burrow."

Telford stared as a drunken man might who had been roused by the glare of a policeman's lantern.

The company looked first at the girl, then at Telford, then at each other. Telford drew a deep sigh.

"My God!" he muttered.

A babel of conversation and chatter broke out. Telford gazed at Elsie Gwyn as if fascinated.

"Listen, everybody."

A hush fell over the stage. It was Elsie Gwyn who spoke. "I asked Mr. Telford to give me a trial as Jenny Burrow. He said that I was not sufficiently experienced and could not create such a part. I thought I could. Of course what I have just said was all— — "

"Fudge and Florrie," broke in Walters, as if to reassert his claims as a comedian.

"Exactly, Mr. Walters. You'll forgive me, won't you?"

"Sure, girl," he said genially. "There's no one here who'll ever want to quarrel with you after to-day," he added, at which there was a laugh.

"Now, Mr. Telford," said Elsie, "can I or can I not play the part of Jenny Burrow?"

"Play it, girl, I should think you could," cried Telford, jumping up from the chair. "But you've given me the fright of my life. Come along upstairs and we'll sign a contract."

The two left the stage together, and the company trooped out after them, knowing that rehearsal was over for that day.

Roger Telford was a sportsman, and too happy at the termination of his nightmare to bear malice. He was delighted to find that his luck had not failed him, and that he had found an actress capable of creating the part that he had found such difficulty in casting.

"She knew some fancy words," was Bindle's comment. "She ought to get on."

"Was she a success?" enquired Sallie eagerly.

"She made the hit of the season," I replied. "Somehow the story leaked out and got into the papers. It was the biggest advertising boom Telford has ever had. The public flocked to see the girl who had scored off Roger Telford."

"A great advertisin' stunt," said Angell Herald. "Wish I'd had it. Some fellows get all the luck."

"She ought to have married him," murmured Sallie, gazing at nothing in particular.

"She did," I said, "last season. It was regarded as her greatest hit."

"Oh! how splendid," cried Sallie, clapping her hands in a way that would seem like gush in anyone else.

Bindle looked gloomy disapproval.

"It's all very well for you miss, but think of 'im an' all them words she knew."

"But, Mr. Bindle, she was an actress," cried Sallie.

"So's every woman, miss. They can't 'elp it."

"Mr. Bindle!" Sallie reproved.

"Think o' that poor chap goin' an' doin' it after wot 'e'd 'eard. Isn't it jest like 'em. Nobody won't believe nothink till they've tried it themselves.

"I 'ad a mate, a real sport 'e was. 'E wouldn't believe me, said 'is little bit o' fluff wasn't like other bits wot I'd seen. 'E talked as if 'e could 'ear 'er feathers a-rustling when the wind blew, poor chap! Then 'e did it."

Bindle paused as if overcome by the memory of his mate's misfortune.

"'E 'adn't 'ad 'er a month when 'e comes round to me one Saturday afternoon. I was sittin' in the back-yard a-listenin' to a canary and wot Mrs. 'Iggins thought of 'er ole man.

"'You was right, Joe,' 'e says, lookin' about as 'appy as a lobster wot 'ears the pot bubblin'.

"'So you don't 'ear the wind through 'er feathers now, Jim?' I says.

"'There never warn't no feathers, Joe,' 'e says, 'only claws. Come an' 'ave a drink?'

"When a cove wot's been talkin' about 'is misses says, 'Come an' 'ave a drink,' you can lay outsider's odds on 'is 'avin' drawn a blank."

"J.B. never admits of the law of exception," remarked Dare. "That is the fundamental weakness of his logical equipment."

"Fancy it bein' all that," remarked Bindle drily.

"As Sallie remarked," continued Dare, "this young woman was an actress, and she was out for an engagement."

"An' got a weddin' thrown in," said Bindle. "Every woman's out for an engagement, an' yer can leave it to them that it ain't goin' to end there. Well, 'ere's for Fulham, an' my little allotment of 'eaven. S'long everybody," and Bindle departed, knowing that as Carruthers was present he would not be required to call a taxi for Sallie.

It was unusual for Bindle to be the first to leave, and we speculated as to the cause. It was Sallie who guessed the reason as Bindle had told her Mrs. Bindle was poorly, having caught "wot Abraham 'ud call a cold on 'er bosom."

CHAPTER XVI
THE MOGGRIDGES' ZEPPELIN NIGHT

"I'm tired," said Bindle one evening, his cheery look belying his words, "tired as Gawd must be of 'Earty." He threw himself into a chair and fanned himself with a red silk pocket-handkerchief.

"What's the trouble, J.B.?" asked Dick Little, handing Bindle his tankard.

Bindle drank deeply and proceeded to light a cigar Windover had handed him. Bindle's taste in tobacco had in the early days of the Night Club caused us some anxiety. One night Windover came in and began to sniff the air suspiciously.

"There's something burning," he announced. We all made ostentatious search for the source of the smell. It was Windover who traced it to Bindle's cigar. Taking it from his hand he had smelt it gingerly and then returned it to its owner.

"I think," he remarked quite casually, "I should change the brand, J.B. We cannot allow you to imperil your valuable life. Your tobacconist has grossly deceived you. That is not a cigar, it's an offence against the constitution."

"Is it really, sir," said Bindle anxiously as he regarded the offending weed. "I thought it 'ad a bit of a bite to it."

Windover had then launched into a lengthy monologue, during which he traced all the evils of the world, from the Plagues of Egypt to the Suffrage Agitation, to the use of questionable tobacco. The upshot had been that Bindle agreed to allow Windover to advise him in such matters in future. That is how it came about that at the Night Club Bindle smokes shilling cigars, for which he pays Windover at the rate of ten shillings a hundred, under the impression that they are purchased for that sum.

I afterwards discovered that the offending smokes were known as "Sprague's Fulham Whiffs," one shilling and threepence for ten in a cardboard box.

"The trouble," remarked Bindle in reply to Dick Little's question, "is that people won't do the right thing. I jest been to see Mrs. Biggs wot's in trouble. Last week ole Sam Biggs shuts the door an' window, turns on the gas, an' kills 'imself, an' leaves 'is missus to pay the gas bill. It's annoyed 'er."

"Is she much upset?" enquired Sallie solicitously.

"Somethink awful, miss. She don't seem to be able to get 'er voice down again, it's got so 'igh tellin' the neighbours. I told 'er that it costs yer money to get rid of most things, from a boil to an 'usband, an' Sam ain't dear at a bit extra on the gas bill."

The sittings of the Night Club invariably began and ended with conversation. Before opening the proceedings by calling for the story, Bindle frequently eases his mind of what was pressing most heavily upon it. His utterances are listened to as are those of no one else. If he be conscious of the fact he does not show it.

He has become a law unto himself. He is incapable of giving offence, because there is nothing but good-nature in his mind.

One of our members, Robert Crofton, a little doctor man, has a most extraordinary laugh, which he seems unable to control. It is something of a cackle punctuated by a quick indrawing of breath. One night after listening attentively to this strange manifestation of mirth, Bindle remarked with great seriousness to Windover:

"No one didn't ought to make that noise without followin' it up with an egg."

From that date Crofton was known as "the Hen."

It took considerable argument before Bindle would agree to the inclusion in this volume of the story of how Mr. Moggridge was cured of his infatuation for Zeppelins.

I

Mr. Josiah Moggridge was haunted by Zeppelins! It is true that he had not seen one, had never even heard a bomb explode, or a gun fired in anger; still he was obsessed with the idea of the "Zeppelin Menace." He read every article and paragraph dealing with the subject in all the newspapers and magazines he came across. His children jackalled industriously for this food for their parent. If Dorothy, who was as pretty as she was romantic, arrived home late, her olive-branch would be some story or article about Zeppelins. If Alan, who was sixteen and endowed with imagination, got into a scrape, it was a Zeppelin "rumour" that got him out of it.

Mr. Moggridge journeyed far and near in search of the destruction caused by these air monsters. Had the British public known what Mr. Moggridge knew "for a fact," the war would have collapsed suddenly. No nation could be expected to stand up against the "frightfulness" that was to come, according to Mr. Moggridge. In regard to Zeppelins the German people themselves were sceptics compared with Mr. Moggridge.

The slightest hint or rumour of a Zeppelin raid would send him off hot-foot in search of the ruin and desolation spread by these accursed contrivances. The Moggridge girls came in for many delightful excursions in consequence, for Mr. Moggridge was never happy unless he had about him some of his numerous progeny. If Irene wanted to see the daffydowndillies in Kew Gardens, it seemed almost an interposition of providence that she should hear there had been a Zeppelin raid near Richmond. In justice to her it must be admitted that she would discredit the rumour; but nothing, not even an Act of Parliament, could turn Mr. Moggridge from the pursuit of his hobby.

No amount of discouragement seemed to affect him. If he drew a blank at Balham, he would set out for Stratford with undiminished ardour. Should Holloway fail him, then Streatham would present the scene of desolation he dreaded, yet sought so assiduously. "Man never is but always to be blest," might have been the motto of Josiah Moggridge.

Mrs. Moggridge was the type of woman who regards her husband as something between a god and a hero. To Mr. Moggridge she herself was always "Mother," and as if in justification of the term, she had presented him with one son, and eight daughters, whose ages ranged from eleven to twenty-two. Having done this Mrs. Moggridge subsided into oblivion. She had done her "bit," to use the expression of a later generation.

Her attitude towards life was that of a hen that has reached the dazzling heights of having produced from thirteen eggs thirteen pullets. She was a comfortable body, as devoid of imagination as an ostrich. Her interests were suburban, her name was Emma, and her waist measurement thirty-eight inches on Sundays and forty-two inches during the rest of the week.

Mr. Moggridge was forever on the alert for the detonation of bombs and the boom of anti-aircraft guns. At night he would listen earnestly for the sound of the trains that passed at the bottom of the Moggridge garden. If the intervals between the dull rumblings seemed too prolonged, he would start up and exclaim, "I believe they've stopped," which as everybody knows meant Zeppelins.

One night after the first Zeppelin raid (it is not permitted by the Defence of the Realm Act to say where or when this occurred, or, for that matter, in what part of the United Kingdom the Moggridges resided), Patricia Moggridge, a petite brunette of twenty, all the Moggridge girls were pretty, enquired, "What shall we do, dad, if Zeppelins come to Cedar Avenue?"

Mr. Moggridge had sat up in sudden alarm. Here was he responsible for the protection of a family, yet he had taken no steps to ensure its safety. Patricia's remark set him thinking deeply. He loved his family, and his family adored him. They regarded him as a child that has to be humoured, rather than a parent who has to be feared. They obeyed him because they wished to see him happy, and Mr. Moggridge's conception of manhood was that "an Englishman's home is his castle."

He was short and round and fussy, as full of interest as a robin, as explosive as a bomb; but with eyes that smiled and a nature that would have warmed an ice-box. A crisis or a misadventure excited him almost to the point of frenzy. Starting for the annual holiday drove him nearly insane with worry lest someone or something be left behind, or they lose the train.

When Patricia asked her innocent question she was sitting on her father's knee "nuzzling his whiskers," as she called it, Mr. Moggridge wore side whiskers and a clean shaven upper lip and chin, she was unaware of what would grow out of her question.

Mr. Moggridge read industriously the advice tendered by various newspapers as to what should be done during a Zeppelin raid. He read with the seriousness of a man who knows that salvation lies somewhere in the columns of the Press.

One night he gathered together the whole of his family in the drawing-room, including the two maids and the cook, and instructed all in what should be done at the sound of the first gun. He made many references to a sheaf of notes and newspaper-cuttings he had before him, which seemed to get terribly mixed. He then enquired if everyone understood; but the half-hearted chorus of "Yeses" that answered him was unconvincing.

"Cook," he said sternly, "what would you do if Zeppelins came?"

"Please, sir, faint," was the reply.

The interrogation of other members of his household convinced him that a further exposition was necessary.

Stripped of their verbal adornments, Mr. Moggridge's instructions were that on the first intimation that Zeppelins were at hand, the whole household was to make for the basement.

Half-an-hour's further "instruction" left everyone still more hopelessly befogged as to what was expected of them. The gist of Mr. Moggridge's instructions was:

(1) That everyone should make for the cellar without bothering about dressing.

(2) That every bath, portable or fixed, tub, jug, or other vessel was each night to be filled with water, and placed on the landings as a protection against incendiary bombs.

(3) That under no circumstances was any light to be turned on (as a precaution Mr. Moggridge turned off the electric light each night) or candle to be lit.

"But how shall we find our way downstairs?" enquired Allan, his son and heir.

"You'll feel it, my boy," replied his father, unconsciously prophetic.

A few days later Mr. Moggridge read of the intention of the Germans to use gas-bombs, and he immediately purchased at Harridges Stores fourteen "Protective Face Masks." That night he returned home feeling that he had saved fourteen lives, including his own.

After dinner the household was once more summoned to the drawing-room, where Mr. Moggridge distributed the gas-masks, and gave a short lecture upon how they were to be worn. When he illustrated his instructions by donning a mask, the younger of the two maids giggled uncontrollably.

Mr. Moggridge glared at her volcanically. "Girl!" he thundered, "do you know that I am trying to save your life."

Whereat the girl burst into tears.

Mr. Moggridge rustled about among his notes anxiously, whilst his hearers watched him with breathless interest. He soon saw that no help was to be expected from the Press, which appeared to be divided into two camps. There was the bomb theory and the gas theory, the one demanding descent and the other ascent.

Mr. Moggridge was nonplussed and referred to the gas-bomb article. Suppose explosive bombs were dropped when they were prepared for gas-bombs and conversely? Suddenly he had an inspiration.

"I've got it!" he shouted, as he danced excitedly from one foot to the other. "If you smell gas you go up to the attics: if you— — "

"But how shall we know it's gas unless we know what it smells like?" questioned Alan.

Mr. Moggridge looked at his only son as at someone who had asked him the riddle of the universe. Alan was notorious for the embarrassing nature of his questions.

"I shall know how to find that out," was all that Mr. Moggridge could reply, and Alan felt that he had obtained a tactical victory.

"In the meantime, if you smell anything you've never smelt before you'll know it's gas."

This seemed to satisfy everyone. Nevertheless, Mr. Moggridge made industrious enquiry as to what gas really smelt like. No one knew; but many theories as to the exact odour were advanced, ranging from vinegar to sewage. At last Mr. Moggridge heard of a man who had actually been gassed. Eagerly he made a pilgrimage to the district in which the hero resided and as eagerly put his question.

"Wot's gas smell like?" remarked the warrior, whose moustache was as yet reluctant down upon his upper lip. "It beats the smell of army cheese 'ollow, an' that's the truth."

And with this Mr. Moggridge had to rest content. In the silent watches of the night, many a member of the Moggridge household would awaken suddenly and sniff expectantly for "a strange odour rather like strong cheese," Mr. Moggridge's paraphrase of the soldier's words.

Mr. Moggridge decided to sleep at the top of the house— alone. He had moved up there and sent down two of the girls to sleep with their mother, because he regarded the upper rooms as the most dangerous, and he was not lacking in courage. He regarded it as his mission in life to protect those who looked to him for protection. In his mind's eye, Mr. Moggridge saw himself the saviour of thirteen lives, possibly fourteen if he had not to give up his own in the attempt.

Each night it was his self-imposed task to examine "the defences" as his daughter, Mollie, called them. On every landing and outside every door were baths, wash-tubs, basins, pails and other vessels containing water. Even when the lights were on, it was a matter of some delicacy to thread one's way through these watery entanglements. The servants grumbled at the additional work involved; but Mr. Moggridge had silenced them with "a Zeppelin bonus," as he called it, and furthermore he had mobilised his whole family to assist in this work of protection against fire.

"When I've saved your worthless lives, you'll be grateful perhaps," he had exploded, and it had taken "Mother" all the next morning to explain to her domestic staff that "valuable" and not "worthless" was the adjective her husband had used.

Outside his own bedroom-door Mr. Moggridge had placed the large dinner gong on which to sound the alarm, and at the head of the stairs an enormous tin-bath full of water. It was so placed that the slightest push would send bath and contents streaming down the stairs. Mr. Moggridge argued that no fire could live in such a deluge.

In time Mr. Moggridge came to regard himself as something between a Sergeant O'Leary and the Roman Sentry, with a leaning towards the sentry; for there would be no reward for him. He saw his family safe and sound, whilst his neighbours lay maimed and dying.

"We are at war, my dears," he would inform his family, "and war is different from peace," and there were none who felt they could question this profound truth.

II

The night of November 5th was bleak and cold and misty, and as Mr. Moggridge prepared for the night he shivered, and prayed that no Zeppelins might come. He disliked the cold intensely, and pictured to himself the unpleasantness of sitting for hours in a damp cellar with very few clothes on. Sleep always came readily to Mr. Moggridge's eyelids, and within five minutes of extinguishing the light and slipping into bed, his heavy breathing announced that he was in the land of wonder that knows and yet does not know a Zeppelin.

How long he had slept Mr. Moggridge had no idea; but he was awakened by what he afterwards described as "a terrific explosion" just beneath his window.

"At last!" was his mental comment as he sprang out of bed, sniffing the air like a cat that smells fish. He rushed to the window and looked out. There were no search lights to be seen; but another explosion, apparently in his own garden sent him bounding from the window to the door. Seizing the handle he tore it open and, grasping the leather-headed hammer, began to pound the dinner-gong as if his salvation depended upon his efforts. "Zeppelins," he yelled, "Zeppelins." There were sounds of doors opening, a babel of voices, a scream and then a soft-padded rush upstairs. "Don't come up here! Go down to the cellar," he shouted and, seizing the gong, he dashed for the stairs. There was another report, and an "Oh my God!" from the cook, followed by a peal of hysterical laughter from the younger of the maids.

There was a yelp, a swiiiiiish of rushing water, a pandemonium of feminine shrieks, a tremendous clatter of metal and crockery, as bath caught pail, and pail overset jug to add to the torrent that rushed down the staircase like a flood. Mr. Moggridge had stumbled against the big bath!

The avalanche caught the Moggridges in the rear, shriek followed agonised shriek, as the cold water struck the slightly clad bodies, the shrieks crystallised into yells of anguish as the baths, jugs and bowls came thundering after the water. It seemed the object of animate and inanimate alike to get to the ground floor first. At each landing there was a momentary pause, just as a wave will poise itself before crashing forward, then more crashes and shrieks and groans. All had lost their foothold, and were inextricably mixed up with baths and bits of crockery. At last the torrent reached the hall, where it lay gasping and choking, wondering if this were death or the after punishment.

"My God!" shrieked Mr. Moggridge. "Gas!"

He had forgotten his mask.

He struggled to rise, but the cook and half a foot-bath were firmly fixed upon his person. He could merely lie and sniff— and pray.

The air was foul with an acrid smell that seemed to have permeated everything. To the Moggridges, heaped on the cold hall-tiles, saturated and bruised, it carried a more conclusive proof of danger than the buffeting received in the dash downstairs. It was Gas! Gas!! Gas!!! They would be ruined for life, even if they escaped death.

Above the wails of the Moggridges and their retainers could be heard explosion after explosion from without. Policemen's whistles were singing their raucous, terrifying note. A female voice was heard laughing and sobbing wildly— the cook was in hysterics, whilst at last from an inextricable heap of human limbs and bodies rose the courageous voice of Mr. Moggridge.

"Keep cool, keep calm," he besought. "You are quite safe here. You've got your gas masks. We— — "

He was interrupted by a heavy and imperious pounding upon the knocker, and a continuous sounding of the spring bell. A disc of light could be seen through the stained-glass windows of the hall. From the shivering heap there was no movement to open the door, nothing but cries and sobs and moans. The pounding continued, punctuated by occasional explosions from without. It was Alan who at last crept out of the corner from which he had watched the avalanche of his family and its servitors, and went to the door, unbolting it and admitting what appeared to be two rays of light. They ferreted about until they fell on the heap of Moggridges.

Alan's first thought had been to turn on the electric light at the meter. He now switched on the hall lights, discovering two policemen and two special constables, who in turn discovered Mr. Moggridge. He had wriggled into a sitting posture, where he remained grasping the dinner gong, as Nero might have grasped his instrument when disaster overtook Rome, surrounded and held down by his progeny.

"Oh, turn off the light, do, please!" pleaded a voice, and there was a chorus of cries and endeavours to make scanty draperies cover opulent limbs; but the water had done its work, and one of the policemen, remembering that he had sisters, turned his head aside, and the "specials," for the first time since they had been enrolled, decided that it wasn't so lacking in incident after all, whilst owners and possessors of Moggridge limbs sought to hide them beneath other Moggridge limbs, and those who could not do so hid their faces.

III

"You done fine!" A happy grin spread itself over the features of the speaker, a little man with a red nose, a green baize apron and a blue and white cricket cap, much the worse for wear. "You done fine," he repeated, and then as if to himself, "Yes, them big crackers do make an 'ell of a row." And Joseph Bindle looked at Alan Moggridge approvingly.

"Wasn't it lucky I went to help Aunt Mary move? If I hadn't I shouldn't have seen you and— — "

"And there wouldn't a been no Zeppelin raid round your way. Well you 'ave to thank Dr. Little for the stuff wot made 'em think it was gas-bombs! Fancy them runnin' in your old dad for lettin' off fireworks. So long, sonny," and with a nod and a grin Bindle passed on, wondering if Mrs. Bindle had stewed-steak and onions for supper.

"Oh! Mr. Bindle!" expostulated Sallie when the story came to an end. Then after a pause she added, "Don't you think it was a little cruel?"

There was concern upon Bindle's face: he was troubled that Sallie should criticise him. He looked from her to me, as if desirous that I should share some of the responsibility. It was the first time I had ever seen Bindle abashed. The dear chap is in reality as tender-hearted as a woman, and it was evident that, for the first time, he saw things as they appeared to Sallie.

"Well, miss," he said at last. "I 'adn't thought of it that way. I'm sorry for them gals," but in spite of himself the flicker of a grin passed across his features. "I was only thinkin' o' the old man wot didn't ought to be allowed to go about scarin' people out o' their senses. I'm sorry, miss," and Bindle really was sorry. For the rest of the evening it was easy to see that he regarded himself as in disgrace. The way in which his eyes kept wandering to where Sallie was sitting, reminded me of a dog that has been scolded, and watches wistfully for the sign that shall tell him all is forgiven.

When Bindle returned from seeing Sallie into her taxi, I could see that the cloud had been brushed aside; for he was once more his old jovial self.

J.B. is a strange creature, as mischievous as a monkey; but as lovable as— well, as a man who is white all through, and as incapable of hurting the helpless as of harming the innocent. He has probably never heard of the Public School Spirit; yet it has not much to teach him about playing the game.

CHAPTER XVII
SALLIE AT THE WHEEL

It is one of Windover's pet theories that if a man will but be natural, he can go anywhere and do anything. He claims that the Public School benefits a man not by what it bestows; but rather by what it destroys.

"It clips the ragged edges of a man's ego," he would remark, "and teaches him that as an entity he has no place in the universe." Windover will talk for hours on this subject. Simplicity of nature and the faculty of adapting himself to any environment are, according to him, the ideal results the Public Schools achieve.

In all probability Bindle never had any ragged edges to his ego. Simple-minded and large-hearted, as much at home with the denizens of Mayfair as the inhabitants of Hounsditch, he seems never at a loss. He is always just Bindle, and that is why everyone seems instinctively to like him. He always does the right thing, because he knows no wrong thing to do. Unlike Angell Herald, he is not burdened with two distinct sets of "manners." Bindle would discuss regicides with Hamlet, or noses with a Cyrano de Bergerac with entire unconsciousness of giving offence. He is one thing to all men, as Dare once told him, whereat Bindle remarked, "But don't forget the ladies, sir."

One Sunday evening, just as the Club was breaking up, Sallie remarked to Bindle, "Next Saturday, Mr. Bindle, you must get a whole day's holiday and come with me for a pic-nic."

"Me, miss?" enquired the astonished Bindle. "Me an' you at a pic-nic. Well I'm blessed."

Bindle was taken by surprise. He looked from Sallie to Windover and then to me, as if seeking an explanation of why Sallie should invite him.

"Just we four," Sallie went on in that inimitable way of hers, which would make purgatory a paradise. "We'll take the car and luncheon and tea-baskets. It will be splendid. You will come Mr. Bindle, won't you?" Sallie looked at him with sparkling eyes.

"Come, miss?" cried Bindle. "Come? I'll come if it costs me Mrs. B.'s love. You did say a motor car, miss?" he enquired anxiously, and Sallie's assurance that she had, seemed all that was necessary to complete his happiness.

That evening Bindle and I left Dick Little's flat together. For some time we walked along in silence, each engaged with his own thoughts. Suddenly Bindle broke the silence.

"Wot did I ought to wear, sir?" he enquired. There was a look of anxiety on his face, and unusual corrugations on his forehead.

"Well, J.B.," I remarked, "you'd look nice in muslin with a picture hat." His reproachful look, however, showed me that I had made a mistake.

"I can't wear them Oxford togs with 'er," he remarked.

It should be explained that when Bindle went to Oxford, impersonating the millionaire uncle of an unpopular undergraduate, he had been fitted out with a wardrobe to suit the part. Included in it were a loud black and white check suit, a white waistcoat, a Homburg hat with a puggaree, a red necktie and a cane heavily adorned with yellow metal. Involuntarily I shuddered at the thought of what Sallie would suffer if Bindle turned up in such a costume.

"No," I said with great seriousness, "they're not quite suited to motoring. You must get a new rig out, J.B.," I added.

Still Bindle's face did not clear, and I guessed that it was a question of finance.

I proffered assistance; but that did not help matters. It seemed to make things worse: Bindle is very independent. For some time we walked along in silence. Suddenly I had an inspiration.

"I'll sell one of your yarns to an unsuspecting editor," I said, "and we'll share the plunder. I'll advance you something on account of your share."

In a second the clouds disappeared.

"You're sure it'll earn enough?" he enquired suspiciously.

I proceed to swear that it would in a manner that would have made Lars Porsena envious. I was interrupted by a taxi pulling up with a grind just behind, and Windover jumped out, paid the man and joined us.

"I quite forget," Windover began. "Sallie told me to arrange to meet at Putney Town Station, she'll run the car through and pick us up there."

Bindle explained to Windover that the question of his wardrobe had been under discussion and the upshot was that Windover, who is a supreme artist in the matter of clothes, undertook to see Bindle properly turned out.

On Saturday morning I was at the appointed place a few minutes before nine, I looked round for Bindle, and then forgot him in watching the struggles of a horse to drag a heavily-laden coal-cart up the rise where the High Street passes over the railway.

The level reached, the carter drew up to the curb where the horse stood quivering and panting, bathed in sweat. Suddenly I became aware that one of the men I had observed pushing behind the cart was Bindle; but such a Bindle. No wonder I had at first failed to recognise a blue-suited, brown-booted, dark-tied Bindle. Everything about him was the perfection of fit and cut, from his simple crook cane to his wash-leather gloves. Most wonderful of all, Bindle carried his clothes as if accustomed to them every day of the week.

With perfect gravity he drew off his right glove before shaking hands.

"D'yer like it, sir?"

I drew a sigh of relief. The vernacular was unchanged; it was still the same Bindle.

"J.B.," I said gravely, "I've never seen a better dressed man in my life. It's an entire metamorphosis.";

"There you're sort o' wrong, sir. It's 'is Lordship. D'yer think she'll like it, sir?" he enquired anxiously.

By "she" I knew he meant Sallie.

"Sure of it," I replied with confidence. Bindle seemed reassured. Suddenly his eye caught the black line across the palm of his right glove.

"Look wot I done." He held out the glove for my inspection as a child might a torn pinafore. "Wot'll she think?" There was anxiety in his voice.

"She'll be rather pleased when I tell her how it happened," I replied, at which his face cleared.

"I wanted a red tie to sort o' give it a bite; but 'e wouldn't 'ave it, so 'ere I am," and Bindle drew on his right glove once more.

"Tell me all about it," I urged. "Those clothes were made in the West-End, I swear."

"Got it first time, sir," he remarked, as he drew from his breast-pocket a suspicious-looking cigar with an enormous red and gold band round its middle.

"Let me cut it for you," I broke in hastily, seizing the weed without waiting for his acquiescence. That band would have killed Sallie, so I ripped it off. As I did so Bindle made a movement as if to stop me, but he said nothing. As I raised my eyes from the operation, I saw his regretful gaze fixed upon the band lying on the pavement, a shameless splash of crimson and of gold.

Bindle lighted his cigar and I manoeuvred to get to windward of him.

"You was talkin' about these 'ere duds, sir," remarked Bindle puffing contentedly at what made me pray for Windover's swift arrival: I do not carry cigars. "You was right, sir."

"In what?" I queried.

"They came from Savile Row, from 'is Lordship's own snips. You should a seen 'is face when 'is Lordship said 'e was out for reach-me-downs for yours truly."

It was easy to visualise the scene. Windover easy, courteous, matter-of-fact. His tailor staggered, yet striving to disguise his astonishment under a veneer of urbanity and "yes-my-lords." Windover is the most perfectly bred creature I have ever met. If he were to order riding breeches for a camel, he would do so in such a way that no one would think of laughing, or even regarding it as strange.

"Took me round 'isself everywhere," continued Bindle. "We got this 'at in Piccadilly, these boots an' gloves in Bond Street, also the tie." Bindle looked round cautiously and then bending a little closer he confided, "I'm silk underneath!" He leaned back upon his stick to see the effect. I smiled. "Wi' funny things round me legs to keep me socks up," and he grinned joyously at the thought of his own splendour.

"What did Mrs. Bindle say?" I enquired.

"'Ush, sir, 'ush! She said about every think she could think of, and a good many things she didn't ought to know. She talked about Mammon, keepin' 'oly the Sabbath day, about Abraham's bosom. Jest fancy a woman married to a man like me a-talkin' about another cove's bosom. Why can't she say chest and be respectable?"

"And what did you say?" I queried.

"Oh!" replied Bindle, "I jest asked 'er wot ole Abraham did when he got a chill, an' if 'e called it a cold on 'is bosom?"

I laughed, but Bindle continued seriously, "She arst me where I'd be if the end of the world was to come sudden like."

Scenting a good rejoinder I enquired what he had said.

"I told 'er to look in the saloon-bar first, an' if I wasn't there to try the bottle-an'-jug department. I come away then. Mrs. B.'s a rummy sort o' send-off for an 'oliday," he soliloquised.

After a pause he added, "I'd like to 'ave jest a peep at 'eaven to see if Gawd is really like wot Mrs. B. says. Seems to me 'e must be like one o' them quick-change coves I seen at the Granville. Ole War-an-Whiskers [the Kayser] says 'E 'elps the Germans to kill kids an' 'ack women about, Mrs. B. says 'e's goin' to give me pickles when I die, an ole 'Earty seems to think 'E's collectin' 'oly greengrocers. There was one parson chap wot told me that 'E was kind an' just, with eyes wot smiled. I don't see 'ow 'e can be the ole bloomin' lot cause— — "

Bindle suddenly broke off, straightened himself, lifted his hat and proceeded to pull off his glove. I turned and saw Sallie bringing her "Mercedes" along at a thumping pace. She bore in towards us and brought the car up in a workmanlike manner. Windover, who was seated behind her, jumped out.

"Cheer-o!" said Bindle.

"Cheer-o!" replied Windover. Probably it was the first time in his life that he had ever used the expression: he is inclined to be a purist.

"You been stealin' a march on us, sir," said Bindle.

"I was literally picked out of my taxi," explained Windover, "hardly given time to pay the man, I should say over-pay the man, I had forgotten the war."

I saw from the look in Sallie's eyes that she was pleased with Bindle's appearance.

"Jump in," she said. Sallie is always brisk and business-like when running "Mercy," as she calls her car.

"You must sit by me, Mr. Bindle."

Bindle's cup of happiness was now full to overflowing. When he took his seat beside Sallie I caught his eye. In it was a look of triumph. It said clearly, "Jest fancy 'er wantin' me when she could have a lord."

As we swung up Putney hill, Windover told me of his experiences in clothing Bindle. At my particular request he also gave me an approximate idea of the sum involved. It was worthy both of Windover and the West End.

"But my dear Windover," I expostulated, "was silk underwear absolutely necessary for this pic-nic?"

Windover turned upon me a pair of reproachful eyes. "Phillips is sensitive," he remarked, "and if he knew that any of his 'creations' were put over anything but silk, he would close my account."

With that I had to rest content. Personally I had seen no need to take Bindle to Phillips at all; but Windover is an artist, he "composes" his wearing-apparel as a painter composes a picture, or a poet a sonnet. If providence be discriminating it will punish Windover in the next world for his misdemeanours in this by making him wear odd socks, or a hard hat with a morning coat. I told him so.

As we talked I noticed Windover snuffing the air like a hound. He looked at me, then moved the rug to see if there were anything at the bottom of the car. Finally he smelt the rug, still he seemed dissatisfied, continuing to turn his head from side to side sniffing, as if endeavouring to trace some evil smell. Finally his eyes fixed themselves on Bindle sitting complacently smoking his cigar.

"Good God!" he muttered as he screwed his eye-glass into his eye. "I thought it was a dead dog. He must have run out of 'coronels.'" I heard him mutter.

"You can't raise a man from Fulham to Curzon Street in a few hours, Windover," I remarked reproachfully. "You taught Bindle to remove his glove before shaking hands, and you also gave him very creditable instructions in how to lift his hat so as not to look like a third rate actor in a Restoration melodrama; but you omitted to instruct him in the choice of cigars."

Windover has as delicate a taste in tobacco as in women; in other words he is extremely fastidious. I watched him as he turned the problem over in his mind. I could follow his train of thought. It was obviously impossible to sit inhaling the fumes of Bindle's cigar. It was unthinkable again to tell the dear chap it was nothing short of a pollution. In all probability it was a threepenny cigar, the extra penny being in honour of the occasion. Therefore some other way out of the difficulty must be devised. I, had every confidence in Windover and his sense of delicacy. His eyeglass dropped from his eye, a sure sign that the strain of deep-thinking was past.

Taking his cigar case from his pocket, he tapped Bindle on the shoulder and whispered to him. Bindle gave a quick look at Sallie, surreptitiously threw away his cigar and accepted one proffered by Windover, the end of which he promptly bit off. Windover sank back into his seat with a sigh, and I saw Bindle turn to Sallie, who changed speed and put on the brakes. He then calmly proceeded to light his new cigar, quite unconscious that, in asking her to stop a car going at nearly forty miles an hour, he had transgressed against one of the "Thou shalt nots" of motoring.

"How did you do it?" I asked Windover.

"I told him that Sallie would be mortally offended if she knew he was smoking one of his own cigars, it was her pic-nic and she had given me some cigars with which to keep him supplied."

Tactful Windover.

Lunch we had in a field well off the main road. Bindle's face was a study as we unpacked the luncheon hamper. Sallie is very thorough, and her pic-nic appointments are the most perfect I have ever encountered, from the folding legless table to the dainty salt-spoons. For once Bindle was silent; but his eyes were busy. When the champagne appeared with the ice and the ice-cream cooler, his emotions overcame him. I heard him mutter to himself, "Well I'm blowed."

During the meal the rest of us talked; but Bindle said little.

"You're very quiet, Mr. Bindle," said Sallie at last, smiling.

"I'm too 'appy to talk, miss," said Bindle with unusual gravity, and there was a look in his eyes that was more eloquent than his words. "You see, miss, you can do this any day yer likes, and yer gets sort o' used to it; but I don't suppose I shall ever do it again, and I want to make sure that I'm enjoyin' every bit of it. I can talk any time."

Sallie turned her head quickly, and I could see that her eyes were moist. Bindle's remark was not without its pathos.

After lunch Sallie took Bindle off for a walk, whilst Windover and I stayed by the car. During the half hour they were absent, only one remark was made as we sat smoking, and that was by Windover.

"I have come to regard Bindle as a social antiseptic," he said.

I knew it had taken Windover since lunch to arrive at this definition.

As the hours sped, Bindle remained silent and Sallie was content to devote herself to the car. Snug in one of Carruthers' motor coats, Bindle devoured with his eyes everything he saw; but what a changed Bindle. There was no cracking jokes, or passing remarks with passers-by. He did not even look at a public-house. Instinctively he had adapted himself to his environment.

"I think he's the most perfect gentle-person I've met," Sallie had once said.

After dinner Bindle became more conversational. It was an evening when the silence could be heard. In the distance was an occasional moan of a train, or the bark of a dog; but nothing else. The sky was clear, the sun was spilling itself in deep gold upon the landscape. The dinner had been good, and within us all was a feeling of content.

"How is Mrs. Bindle?" enquired Sallie of Bindle.

"Oh jest ordinary like, miss. 'Er soul still gives 'er a lot o' trouble."

"Don't you think," said Sallie with that smile of hers which seemed to disarm her remark of the criticism it contained, "that you sometimes tease her too much?"

Bindle's grin faded. "I been thinkin' that too, miss," he said seriously. "But some'ow the things seem to come out, an' I don't mean 'er no 'arm really, miss."

"I'm sure you don't," Sallie hastened to say.

"Well, take last night, for instance," said Bindle. "We was talkin' about the German Corpse Factory. I'd been readin' to 'er from the paper 'ow they turned the poor devils wot 'ad died doin' their bit to kill our chaps into marjarine, candles, oils for motor-cars, and that sort o' stuff. We was 'aving supper an' I 'appens to say quite innocent like: 'If you an' me was 'Uns, Lizzie and poor ole 'Earty 'ad died for 'is country, a thing wot 'Earty never will do if 'e can 'elp it, we might be a'spreadin' of 'im on this 'ere bread, and that there candle might be a bit of 'Earty an' us not knowin' it.' Well, there ain't much 'arm in that miss, is there? Yet she said I'd spoilt 'er supper, an' she pushed the salmon away from 'er an' said I wasn't fit to live with, an' that I'd got a dirty mind."

"J.B.," said Windover. "My sympathies are entirely with Mrs. Bindle. Your remark was extremely inappropriate."

Bindle looked round him from one to another. "Well, sir," he expostulated, "wasn't I right?"

"It was not a question of right, J.B.," said Windover, with mock severity. "It was a question of tact."

"Tack!" said Bindle. "'Adn't I taken 'ome a tin of salmon, and when the breeze started didn't I whistle 'er favourite 'ymn GOSPEL BELLS? Look 'ere, sir, I ain't got much to learn in the way of tack wi' women."

"You see," said Sallie gently, "a remark like that sometimes turns people against their food."

"Yes, miss," said Bindle, "that may be; but if you're a German you never know what you're spreadin' on your bread. It may be your uncle, or it may be somebody else's uncle, an' that's worse still."

"Mr. Bindle," cried Sallie, "if you say another word about anything so horrible I shall— I shall— well, I shall drive on and leave you alone in the field."

"I'm sorry, miss," said Bindle with great seriousness. "I didn't know that you— that you— — "

"That I was like Mrs. Bindle," interpolated Sallie.

"Good Lord! miss, you ain't like 'er."

"Well, let's change the subject," said Sallie smiling, "or I shan't be able to eat for a week."

"But it didn't really spoil 'er supper, miss," said Bindle earnestly. "She finished the salmon."

For some time we continued to smoke in silence.

"Funny thing, religion," remarked Bindle at last, a propos of nothing; "it seems to get different people different ways. Now 'Earty and Mrs. B., they seem to think Gawd is near 'em in that smelly little chapel o' theirs; as for me this is what makes me think o' Gawd." And Bindle waved the hand holding his cigar to embrace everything about us.

"But why," enquired Windover wickedly, "should a cigar make you feel nearer to God?"

Bindle turned to Windover and looked him straight in the eyes.

"I wasn't jokin', sir," he said simply.

"I beg your pardon, J.B.," and there was a something in Windover's tone which showed that he regarded the reproof as merited.

"If I was startin' a religion," continued Bindle, "I'd 'ave people go out in the country, an' kneel down in a field, an' look up at the sky when the sun was shinin'. They'd get a better idea o' Gawd than wot 'Earty and Mrs. B.'s got."

"You're a sun-worshipper then," said Sallie.

"Jest fancy anyone who made all this," Bindle's eyes roamed about him, "wantin' to grill a poor cove like me because I ain't done all the things I ought to a' done."

"But," said Sallie, "don't you think that everybody has their own idea of God?"

"Yes, miss," said Bindle. "But they want to ram their own ideas down everybody else's throat. I see in the paper the other day, when we brought a Zepp. down, that they buried all the poor chaps wot was burnt together. They're 'Uns," he added; "but you can't 'elp feelin' sorry for wot they 'ad to suffer. They 'ad a clergyman an' a Catholic priest, to read the burial service over them. The papers said the priest was there in case some of the dead 'Uns was Catholics. It looks as if a chap 'adn't got a chance of goin' to heaven unless 'e sort of got a ticket from the parson of 'is own church."

Someone has described Anatole France as "a pagan preoccupied with Christ." The same description applies to Joseph Bindle. He cannot keep long off the subject of religion, and in all his comments there seems to be the same instinctive groping for light.

"'Earty reminds me of a cove I used to know wot never seemed to get thirsty except when 'e saw a pub; well, 'Earty never seems to feel religious except when 'e sees a chapel, then it sort o' comes over 'im. If 'e really feels 'e wants to pray, why can't 'e kneel down beside 'is own 'taters. If there's a Gawd, 'e's just as much in a greengrocer's shop as in a dirty little tin chapel, that's wot I says." Bindle looked round as if defying contradiction.

"I think you are right," said Sallie; "but you must not forget that Mr. Hearty does not share your views, any more than you share his. If religion helps people to do good, it doesn't much matter when they get it, or where they get it from."

"Yes, miss, but does it 'elp? You remember when the Lusitania went down, well there was a pretty good scrap round Fulham way. One night they went for a poor chap wot 'ad got a German name, an' they wrecked 'is shop. They'd jest got 'old o' 'im, when a big chap comes up wot's done time more'n once an' tells 'em to chuck it.

"'But 'e's an 'Un,' yells the crowd.

"'Yus, but there's only one o' 'im and there's 'undreds o' you,' says Bill, an' as they wouldn't chuck it Bill let fly, an' there was a pretty old mess."

There was silence for a full minute broken at last by Bindle.

"Don't you think Gawd likes a man to do wot Bill did, miss?" enquired Bindle ingenuously.

"I am sure he did," said Sallie, "and what did you do?"

"Oh, I got a black eye, an' Mrs. B. said she was more sure than ever that 'ell was waitin' for me.

"Wot does me about religion," continued Bindle after a pause, "is wot people'll swallow. There's Mrs. B. now: she can't take a pill without a bucket o' water an' about a dozen tries, looks like an 'en 'avin' a drink, she does; yet tell 'er it's religion an' she'd swallow anythink, an' make believe she likes it. If that whale 'adn't been religious, 'e'd never 'ave got Jonah down."

Bindle paused and for a few moments watched a trail of white smoke from a distant train.

"There was a cove somewhere in the bible called 'Fairy.'"

"Pharaoh, King of Egypt," murmured Windover.

"That's 'im, sir," cried Bindle. "Well look 'ow they say Gawd treated 'im."

"I'm afraid I've forgotten," I said with guile.

"Well," began Bindle, settling himself down for a story, "'E took to collectin' Jews, sort o' got 'old of all there was in the market, same as them Americans wi' food. One day the Jews got a-talkin' to each other about 'ome, though I never see a Jew yet wot wanted to get 'ome when 'e could stay in someone else's backyard."

Bindle paused to suck vigorously at his cigar, which showed signs of going out.

"Pharaoh said there wasn't nothin' doin', an' they couldn't go. Though 'ow anyone can want to keep a Jew wot is willin' to go 'ome does me.

"Then the Jews prayed to Gawd, and 'E made Pharaoh say 'e'd let 'em go. Then 'E 'ardened Pharaoh's 'eart an' started givin' Pharaoh beans."

"Was it not boils?" murmured Windover, examining the tip of his cigarette with great intentness.

"Maybe, sir. Well, first Gawd made Pharaoh agree to let the Jews catch the next bus, then 'E strafed 'im, 'ardening the poor ole chap's 'eart till 'e didn't know where 'e was. Wot I say is it wasn't sportin'."

"I'm afraid you cannot judge bible history by Queensberry rules," said Windover.

"It's like lettin' a bird go and then pullin' it back by a bit o' string tied to its leg. Poor ole Pharaoh couldn't 'elp 'isself with Gawd a-'ardenin' of 'is 'eart. That's wot I don't like."

"Your theology is a trifle unconventional, I fear," said Windover. "Where did you learn about Pharaoh?"

"Yer can't live wi' Mrs. B., sir, without pickin' up a lot about 'eaven an' 'arps an' things," was the reply.

"Go on, Mr. Bindle," said Sallie.

"Well, miss," proceeded Bindle. "There's somethink about visitin' sins on children an' grand-children. I 'ad that out with 'Earty one night. 'Earty don't like talkin' religion wi' me. 'E says I ain't got no faith."

"What happened?" Sallie enquired.

"Well, I asked 'Earty why Gawd should punish a man for wot 'is father did."

"'Because,' says 'Earty, "e 'ad an 'ard 'eart, and wouldn't believe in Gawd.'

"'Wot 'ud you say, 'Earty,' I says, 'if the police was to pinch you 'cause your father flitted without 'avin' paid 'is rent?' O' course 'Earty says nothink to that; but mutters that we can't understand the ways o' Gawd.

"Them ain't the ways of Gawd, it's the things these chaps says about 'Im. When you're strong, yer don't go knockin' over things wot can't 'it back. I knew a bruiser once, an' 'e was as gentle as a lamb. I seen a chap want 'im to fight, an' 'e wouldn't, 'cause 'e was afraid of 'urtin'."

Bindle paused to relight his cigar, then when it was once more in full blast he continued:

"Then they tells yer to love yer neighbours as yourself. I'd like 'em to look out of our window when Sandy 'Iggins an' 'is missus is scrappin' in their back-yard. No," he remarked meditatively, "a religion like that's wasted on Fulham."

That is just Bindle, bringing down the divine to the level of men's eyes: and raising the earthly to the mountain tops.

It was nearly one o'clock on Sunday morning when the car slid from the Fulham road into the street that leads to Fenton Street. When we pulled up, Bindle slipped out of Carruthers' overcoat and got down. As he said good-night to Sallie we heard him whisper:

"I never 'ad a day like this before, miss."

We continued on our way in silence. When Sallie dropped me into a passing taxi, Windover remarked:

"I hope I shall be dead when Democracy discovers all it has been denied."

I knew he was referring to Bindle's remark to Sallie.

THE END

DETAILED HISTORICAL CONTEXT

During the period this book was originally written, the world was a very different place. The events of the time produced an impact on the authorship, style and content of this work. In order for you the reader to better appreciate and connect with this book, it is therefore important to have some context on world events during this timeframe. To this end, we have included a detailed events calendar for the 20th century for your reference.

Please give consideration in particular to the era around 1917 the year in which this work was first published.

Disclaimer: Some scenes throughout history may not be suitable for children, for example, in relation to war or violence. Please use your own discretion before reading this section to your child or allowing your child to read it.

THE TWENTIETH CENTURY INTRODUCTION

The 20th century witnessed transformative historical events that left an indelible mark on both the world and literature. The World Wars, the Great Depression, and the collapse of empires reshaped society and its written expressions. Additionally, scientific and technological progress played a significant role in shaping the literary landscape. After World War I, new and unsettling poetry styles like Imagism and Modernism emerged, reflecting the aftermath of the conflict. The interwar period witnessed the rise of Modernism, while post-World War II brought about responses such as Postmodernism. These shifts represented a departure from Victorian literature, as new movements like Georgian and Aestheticism gained prominence. It is essential to grasp this historical backdrop to fully comprehend the books that emerged during the 20th century and their development within this context.

MOVEMENTS AND LITERATURE

A Transition into Modernism

As the 20th century began, there was a noticeable dissatisfaction with the rigid beliefs and conservative values of the Victorian era. The death of Queen Victoria in 1901 and the ascension of Edward VII marked a shift towards a new era characterized by change and uncertainty. Influential thinkers like Albert Einstein, Charles Darwin, Sigmund Freud, Friedrich Nietzsche, and Karl Marx challenged traditional beliefs, profoundly impacting Western culture and our understanding of ourselves and our origins.

H.G. Wells: Pioneering Modernism and Anticipating the Future

In this new era filled with both hope and unease, H.G. Wells, an English writer, delved into the potential effects of scientific and technological progress in his early Utopian works. Through books like "Anticipations of the Reaction of Mechanical and Scientific Progress upon Human Life and Thought" (1901), "Mankind in the Making" (1903), and "Utopia" (1905), Wells explored the transformative power of science and foresaw its impact on human life and society.

Realism Gives Way to Social Commentary in Literature

The Edwardian era witnessed a departure from the aestheticism of the late 19th century, which championed "Art for Art's Sake." Writers like Dante Gabriel Rossetti, Oscar Wilde, and Algernon Charles Swinburne moved away from pure aestheticism and instead used their works as platforms for discussions on pressing social and moral concerns of the time. Playwrights such as George Bernard Shaw, John Galsworthy, and Harley Granville Barker embraced realism and naturalistic techniques, influenced by 19th-century dramatists like Ibsen, Balzac, and Dickens, to critique societal hypocrisies and explore themes of industry, class, and ethics.

Transition and Traditionalism: Bridging the Victorian and Edwardian Eras

Authors like Thomas Hardy, Rudyard Kipling, and G.K. Chesterton straddled the Victorian and Edwardian eras, upholding traditional literary forms and approaches while embracing new ideas. A.E. Housman's pastoral poetry also reflected attempts to revive conventional techniques and themes. The Georgian poets, including Rupert Brooke, Robert Graves, and Edmund Blunden, continued to adopt a more conventional style, blending romantic and emotional elements into their works.

Henry James and Joseph Conrad: Bridging Realism and Modernism

Henry James, an American-born British author, played a crucial role in bridging the gap between realism and modernism. His novels, including "The Wings of the Dove," "The Ambassadors," and "The Golden Bowl," published between 1902 and 1904, expressed a sense of foreboding and despair about a changing world where traditional social structures and moral certainties were fading. Similarly, Joseph Conrad's works like "Heart of Darkness" (1902), "Nostromo" (1907), and "Under Western Eyes" (1911) delved into the consequences of human flaws and arrogance, reflecting a profound disillusionment with the state of the world.

MODERNISM

Literary Exploration and Innovation

The early 20th century marked a period of literary exploration and innovation as writers sought to break away from the post-Romantic traditions of the previous century. Influenced by new philosophical, political, and scientific perspectives, they embraced modernism and its distinctive characteristics.

The Imagist Movement: Embracing Experimentation

The imagists, a group of English and American poets united under the principles advocated by Ezra Pound, exemplified the new modernist attitude. Poets like T. E. Hulme, Richard Adlington, Hilda Doolittle, and Amy Lowell experimented with forms and free verse in their poetry, pushing the boundaries of traditional poetic structures. They sought to capture vivid and precise images with concise language, focusing on the power of imagery and the sensory experience.

Novelists Embrace Innovation

Alongside the poets, novelists also embraced innovation in their works. D.H. Lawrence and James Joyce, for example, employed groundbreaking narrative techniques to convey the complexities and disillusionment of the post-war world. Lawrence explored themes of human sexuality, nature, and modernity in works like "Lady Chatterley's Lover" and "Sons and Lovers." Joyce, on the other hand, famously used stream-of-consciousness narration and intricate linguistic experiments in novels such as "Ulysses" and "Finnegans Wake."

World War I Leaves its Mark on Literature

The experience of World War I had a profound impact on literature. Poets like Rupert Brooke, Wilfred Owen, and Siegfried Sassoon expressed the camaraderie, moral dilemmas, and horrors of war through their powerful and evocative verses. Their works captured the brutal realities of conflict and questioned the established notions of patriotism and heroism. However, it was only in the 1930s that many of these works gained recognition as the full extent of the war's impact began to be comprehended.

T.S. Eliot and the Fragmented Modernist Poetry

T.S. Eliot emerged as a central figure in the modernist poetry movement. His fragmented and allusive style captured the disillusionment and spiritual emptiness of the post-war era. In his landmark poem "The Waste Land" and other works like "Prufrock and Other Observations," Eliot blended mythology, symbolism, and cultural references to explore the fragmented nature of modern existence and the human condition.

Post-World War II Literature: Quest for Meaning

Following World War II, there was a renewed longing for spiritual connection and existential meaning. Authors and poets like W.H. Auden, T.S. Eliot, Evelyn Waugh, and Christopher Fry delved into themes of existentialism, morality, and faith in their works. They reflected the desire for a sense of purpose and significance in a post-war world scarred by the horrors of the conflict.

The Novel in the Post-War Period

The post-war period witnessed the publication of significant novels that addressed various social, cultural, and political concerns. Anthony Powell's monumental cycle of novels, "A Dance to the Music of Time," offered a panoramic view of British society and its changing values over several decades. George Orwell's dystopian classic, "1984," warned of the dangers of totalitarianism and pervasive surveillance.

Other notable works from this period included William Golding's "Lord of the Flies," Muriel Spark's "The Prime of Miss Jean Brodie," and Anthony Burgess's "A Clockwork Orange."

KEY HISTORICAL EVENTS
The 20th century was marked by numerous significant events that shaped the course of history and influenced literature:

Archduke Ferdinand Assassination: The assassination of Archduke Franz Ferdinand in 1914 triggered World War I, leading to a global conflict that reshaped politics and society.

World War I: This devastating war, lasting from 1914 to 1918, involved major powers and resulted in widespread destruction and loss of life.

Russian Revolution: The 1917 revolution in Russia led to the overthrow of the Tsarist autocracy and the rise of the Bolsheviks, ultimately resulting in the formation of the Soviet Union.

Great Depression: The stock market crash of 1929 led to a severe economic downturn known as the Great Depression, causing widespread unemployment and economic instability.

World War II: From 1939 to 1945, World War II engulfed the world, involving major powers and alliances. The Axis powers, led by Nazi Germany, Fascist Italy, and Imperial Japan, faced off against the Allies, including the United States, the Soviet Union, and the United Kingdom. The war brought immense devastation, loss of life, and the Holocaust, leading to the eventual defeat of the Axis powers and a reshaping of the geopolitical landscape.

Cold War: The tensions between the Soviet Union and the United States following World War II resulted in the Cold War. Lasting from the late 1940s to the early 1990s, this ideological conflict and geopolitical rivalry shaped global politics, leading to proxy wars, arms races, and the space race. The Cold War eventually ended with the dissolution of the Soviet Union.

Civil Rights Movement: The mid-20th century witnessed a significant push for civil rights and racial equality in the United States. Led by figures like Martin Luther King Jr., African Americans fought against segregation, discrimination, and for voting rights. The Civil Rights Movement gained momentum in the 1950s and 1960s, leading to important legislation such as the Civil Rights Act of 1964 and the Voting Rights Act of 1965.

Decolonization: The 20th century saw the dismantling of colonial empires as many nations in Africa, Asia, and the Caribbean gained independence. Colonized peoples and nationalist movements fought for self-determination, leading to the formation of new nations and a reshaping of global power dynamics.

These key historical events influenced literature and reflected the changing social, political, and cultural landscapes of the time. The 20th century was also marked by other significant occurrences, including the space race, the rise of feminism, the advent of the internet, and advancements in technology and medicine. Each of these events and movements played a role in shaping the world as we know it today, leaving a lasting impact on literature and human history.

This concludes the historical context.

Thank you for your interest in our publications. Please don't forget to check out our other books and leave a review if you enjoyed this book.

Printed in Great Britain
by Amazon

44743559R00108